WINTER WARMERS

add warmth and beauty to wintertime with the **rustic charm of homemade quilts!** Along with some coordinating pillows and other accessories, the 14 old-fashioned blankets will wrap you and your loved ones in homespun comfort. Whether you're reading by the fireplace or taking a sleigh ride through freshly fallen snow, our classic **quilts are ideal for keeping you toasty.**

The timeless appeal of these patchwork pretties endures today to remind us of the love and warmth that is the heart of the home. We've taken some of the most beloved **heirloom patterns** and combined them with our **time-saving techniques,** so you can recapture the simple pleasures of yesteryear in a fraction of the time it took earlier generation quilters.

Whether you're a master quilter or a novice, you'll love this collection of cold-weather warmers. The **easy-to-follow instructions** will have you quilting your own cozy creations in no time.

LEISURE ARTS, INC.
Little Rock, Arkansas

1

Production: Lisa Lancaster
Editorial: Suzie Puckett
Art: Dana Vaughn

We extend a sincere *thank you* to the following people who assisted in making some of the quilts in this book: Pat Eaton; Glenda Taylor; and the Gardner Memorial United Methodist Church Quilters, North Little Rock, Arkansas: Elois Allain, Leon Dickey, Fredda McBride, Carol Pittman, Edna Sikes, Betty Smith, Esther Starkey, Thelma Starkey, and Inez Wheat.

TABLE OF CONTENTS

roman stripe

This striking quilt will provide a welcome spot of color on a frosty winter day. Known as Roman Stripe when pieced using print fabrics, the classic pattern is more commonly called Sunshine and Shadows among the Amish of the Midwest. Quilters in these communities traditionally use only solid fabrics for the stripes with black as the background. For our Roman Stripe quilt, we selected a variety of plaids — using black for the solid triangles helps blend the tones beautifully! To create the striped sections, we rotary cut strip-pieced sets using a special ruler that produces accurate angles with ease. The fast and simple pattern, completed with basic borders, is a delightful project for any first-time quilter.

4

ROMAN STRIPE QUILT

SKILL LEVEL: 1 2 3 4 5
BLOCK SIZE: 7" x 7"
QUILT SIZE: 78" x 92"

YARDAGE REQUIREMENTS

Yardage is based on 45"w fabric.

- 4⅝ yds of black plaid
- 2¾ yds **total** of assorted plaids
- 2⅛ yds of red plaid
- 1⅞ yds of black solid
  7¼ yds for backing
  1 yd for binding
  90" x 108" batting

You will also need:
  Companion Angle™ Rotary Cutting Ruler (made
    by EZ International)

CUTTING OUT THE PIECES

All measurements include a ¼" seam allowance. Follow
Rotary Cutting, *page 112, to cut fabric.*

1. **From black plaid:**
   - Cut 2 lengthwise strips 12¼" x 82" for
     top/bottom outer borders.
   - Cut 2 lengthwise strips 12¼" x 72" for **side outer
     borders**.

2. **From assorted plaids:**
   - Cut a total of 44 **strips** 1¾"w.

3. **From red plaid:**
   - Cut 2 lengthwise strips 2¾" x 67" for **side inner
     borders**.
   - Cut 2 lengthwise strips 2¾" x 58" for **top/bottom
     inner borders**.

4. **From black solid:**
   - Cut 7 strips 7⅞"w. From these strips, cut 32
     squares 7⅞" x 7⅞". Cut squares once diagonally
     to make 64 **triangles** (you will need 63 and have
     1 left over).

square (cut 32)

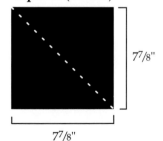

7⅞"

7⅞"

triangle (cut 64)

ASSEMBLING THE QUILT TOP

Follow ***Piecing and Pressing***, *page 114, to make quilt top.*

1. Sew 4 **strips** together in random color order to
   make **Strip Set**. Make 11 **Strip Sets**.

Strip Set (make 11)

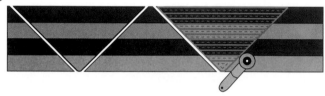

2. Aligning top and bottom edges of ruler with long
   edges of strip set, use Companion Angle ruler to
   cut 63 **Unit 1's** from **Strip Sets**, turning ruler 180°
   after each cut (**Fig. 1**).

Fig. 1

Unit 1 (make 63)

3. Sew 1 **Unit 1** and 1 **triangle** together to make
   Block. Make 63 **Blocks**.

Block (make 63)

4. Sew 7 **Blocks** together to make **Row**. Make 9
   Rows.

Row (make 9)

5. Referring to **Quilt Top Diagram**, sew **Rows** together to make center section of quilt top.
6. Follow **Adding Squared Borders**, page 117, to sew **side**, then **top** and **bottom inner borders** to center section. Add **side**, then **top** and **bottom outer borders** to complete **Quilt Top**.

COMPLETING THE QUILT
1. Follow **Quilting**, page 118, to mark, layer, and quilt, using **Quilting Diagram** as a suggestion. Our quilt is machine quilted.
2. Cut a 34" square of binding fabric. Follow **Binding**, page 122, to bind quilt using 2¹/₂"w bias binding with mitered corners.

Quilting Diagram

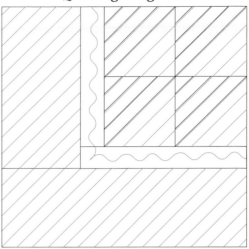

Quilt Top Diagram

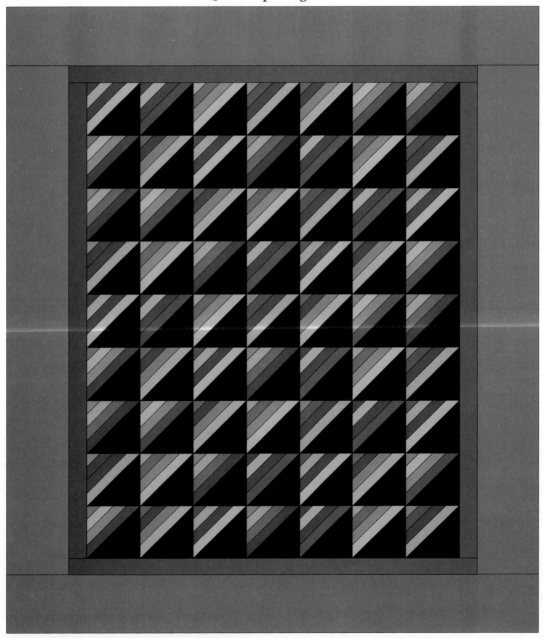

hour-glasses and geese

*f*locks of geese flying south for the winter signal that it's time to snuggle under a cozy quilt. This impressive cover is a delightful combination of bold Hourglass blocks set with Flying Geese sashing for a spectacle of pieced triangles. To make the quilt blocks, we used a quick triangle-square method that produces two units at one time. Another easy process, our "sew and flip" technique is a fast and accurate way to create precise points for the Flying Geese units. The design is complemented with basic echo quilting, and the edges are simply finished with plain bias binding.

HOURGLASSES AND GEESE QUILT

SKILL LEVEL: 1 2 3 4 5
BLOCK SIZE: $8\frac{1}{4}$" x $8\frac{1}{4}$"
QUILT SIZE: 81" x 92"

YARDAGE REQUIREMENTS

Yardage is based on 45"w fabric.

☐ $6\frac{7}{8}$ yds of cream print
■ $2\frac{1}{8}$ yds of dark red print
■ $1\frac{3}{8}$ yds of green print
◨ $\frac{5}{8}$ yds of each of 5 assorted prints
  $7\frac{1}{2}$ yds for backing
  1 yd for binding
  90" x 108" batting

CUTTING OUT THE PIECES

All measurements include a $\frac{1}{4}$" seam allowance. Follow
Rotary Cutting, *page 112, to cut fabric.*

1. **From cream print:** ☐
   • Cut 7 strips $9\frac{1}{2}$"w. From these strips, cut 28 **squares** $9\frac{1}{2}$" x $9\frac{1}{2}$".

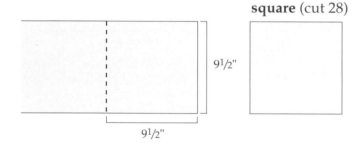

square (cut 28)

$9\frac{1}{2}$"

$9\frac{1}{2}$"

   • Cut 83 strips $1\frac{7}{8}$"w. From these strips, cut 1,812 **small squares** $1\frac{7}{8}$ x $1\frac{7}{8}$".

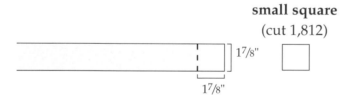

small square
(cut 1,812)

$1\frac{7}{8}$"

$1\frac{7}{8}$"

2. **From dark red print:** ■
   • Cut 7 strips $9\frac{1}{2}$"w. From these strips, cut 28 **squares** $9\frac{1}{2}$" x $9\frac{1}{2}$".

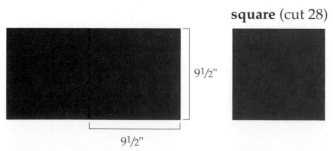

square (cut 28)

$9\frac{1}{2}$"

$9\frac{1}{2}$"

3. **From green print:** ■
   • Cut 13 strips $3\frac{1}{4}$"w. From these strips, cut 271 **green rectangles** $1\frac{7}{8}$" x $3\frac{1}{4}$".

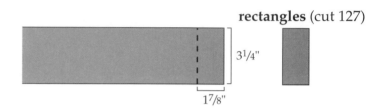

rectangles (cut 271)

$3\frac{1}{4}$"

$1\frac{7}{8}$"

4. **From each of five assorted prints:** ◨
   • Cut 6 strips $3\frac{1}{4}$"w. From these strips, cut 127 **rectangles** $1\frac{7}{8}$" x $3\frac{1}{4}$".

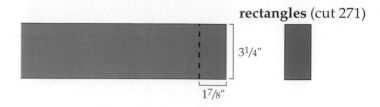

rectangles (cut 127)

$3\frac{1}{4}$"

$1\frac{7}{8}$"

ASSEMBLING THE QUILT TOP

Follow **Piecing and Pressing**, *page 114, to make quilt top.*

1. To make triangle-squares, place 1 dark red print and 1 cream print **square** right sides together. On wrong side of cream square, draw a diagonal line in one direction; stitch $\frac{1}{4}$" from each side of line (**Fig. 1**). Cut apart on drawn line to make 2 **triangle-squares**. Press open, pressing seam allowance toward darker fabric. Repeat with remaining square to make a total of 56 **triangle-squares**.

Fig. 1

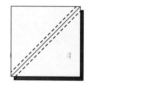

triangle-square (make 56)

2. Referring to **Fig. 2**, place 2 **triangle-squares** right sides and opposite colors together, matching seams. Referring to **Fig. 3**, draw a diagonal line. Stitch 1/4" from each side of line. Cut apart on drawn line and press open to make 2 **Blocks**. Repeat with remaining **triangle-squares** to make a total of 56 **Blocks**.

Fig. 2

Fig. 3

Block (make 56)

3. Place 1 **small square** on 1 **rectangle** and stitch diagonally as shown in **Fig. 4**. Trim 1/4" from stitching line as shown in **Fig. 5**. Press open, pressing seam allowance toward darker fabric.

Fig. 4

Fig. 5

4. Place 1 **small square** on opposite end of **rectangle**. Stitch diagonally as shown in **Fig. 6**. Trim 1/4" from stitching line as shown in **Fig. 7**. Press open, pressing seam allowance toward darker fabric to make **Unit 1**.

Fig. 6

Fig. 7

Unit 1

5. Repeat Steps 3 and 4 using remaining **small squares** and **rectangles** to make a total of 906 **Unit 1's**.

6. Sew 2 **Unit 1's** together to make **Sashing Square**. Make 72 **Sashing Squares**.

Sashing Square (make 72)

7. Sew 6 **Unit 1's** together to make **Sashing Unit**. Make 127 **Sashing Units**.

Sashing Unit (make 127)

8. Sew 8 **Sashing Squares** and 7 **Sashing Units** together to make **Sashing Row**, page 12. Make 9 **Sashing Rows**.

9. Sew 8 **Sashing Units** and 7 **Blocks** together to make **Row**, page 12. Make 8 **Rows**.

10. Referring to **Quilt Top Diagram**, page 13, sew **Sashing Rows** and **Rows** together to complete **Quilt Top**.

Sashing Row (make 9)

Row (make 8)

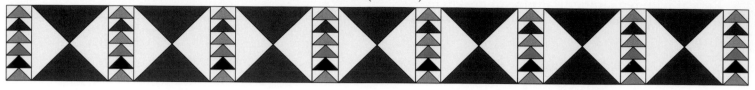

COMPLETING THE QUILT

1. Follow **Quilting**, page 118, to mark, layer, and quilt, using **Quilting Diagram** as a suggestion. Our quilt is hand quilted.

2. Cut a 32" square of binding fabric. Follow **Binding**, page 122, to bind quilt using 2½"w bias binding with mitered corners.

Quilting Diagram

Quilt Top Diagram

clay's choice

Chase away winter chills with this bold blanket and wall hanging. The Clay's Choice quilt pattern is a striking design honoring the valiant resolve of Henry Clay, a respected Kentucky statesman of the 1800's who was committed to preserving the Union. He played a key role in reaching the Missouri Compromise and the Compromise of 1850, but his opposition to slavery ultimately cost him his dream of the presidency. He stood firm in his convictions, stating, "I would rather be right than be president." For our calico version of the traditional design, we used easy grid-pieced triangle-squares to create the simple stars. Plain borders of print fabric are offset with an inner border of small squares set on point.

14

CLAY'S CHOICE QUILT

SKILL LEVEL: 1 2 3 4 5
BLOCK SIZE: 8" x 8"
QUILT SIZE: 91" x 107"

Because of the quick methods used to duplicate the scrappy look of our quilt, you will have some pieces left over after assembling the blocks.

YARDAGE REQUIREMENTS

Yardage is based on 45"w fabric.

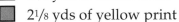

- 6 7/8 yds of black print
- 4 7/8 yds of cream solid
- 2 1/8 yds of yellow print
- 3/4 yd *each* of 2 red, 2 blue, and 2 green prints
  8 1/4 yds for backing
  1 yd for binding
  120" x 120" batting

CUTTING OUT THE PIECES

All measurements include a 1/4" seam allowance. Follow Rotary Cutting, page 112, to cut fabric.

1. **From black print:**
   - Cut 6 strips 22"w. From these strips, cut 12 **rectangles** 16" x 22" for triangle-squares.
   - Cut 2 lengthwise **side outer borders** 3 1/2" x 104".
   - Cut 2 lengthwise **top/bottom outer borders** 3 1/2" x 94".
   - Cut 2 lengthwise **side inner borders** 3 1/2" x 92".
   - Cut 2 lengthwise **top/bottom inner borders** 3 1/2" x 82".

2. **From cream solid:** ☐
   - Cut 25 strips 2 1/2"w. From these strips, cut 396 **small squares** 2 1/2" x 2 1/2".
   - Cut 3 strips 22"w. From these strips, cut 6 **rectangles** 16" x 22" for triangle-squares A's.
   - Cut 7 strips 4 1/4"w. From these strips, cut 59 squares 4 1/4" x 4 1/4". Cut squares twice diagonally to make 236 **border triangles**.

3. **From yellow print:** ▨
   - Cut 25 strips 2 1/2"w. From these strips, cut 396 **small squares** 2 1/2" x 2 1/2".

4. **From red, blue, and green prints:** ◪
   - Cut 2 strips 2 5/8"w from *each* fabric. From these strips, cut a total of 118 **border squares** 2 5/8" x 2 5/8".
   - Cut 1 **rectangle** 16" x 22" from *each* fabric for triangle-square B's.

ASSEMBLING THE QUILT TOP

Follow Piecing and Pressing, page 114, to make quilt top.

1. To make triangle-square A's, place 1 black and 1 cream **rectangle** right sides together. Referring to **Fig. 1**, follow **Making Triangle-Squares**, page 115, to make 70 **triangle-square A's**. Repeat with remaining black and cream **rectangles** to make a total of 420 **triangle-squares A's**. (You will need a total of 396 **triangle-square A's**.)

Fig. 1

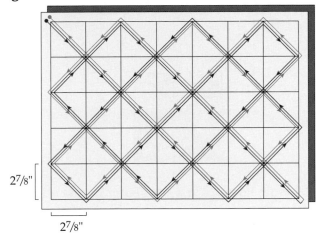

2 7/8"

2 7/8"

triangle-square A (make 420)

2. To make triangle-square B's, place 1 red and 1 black **rectangle** right sides together. Referring to **Fig. 1**, this page, follow **Making Triangle-Squares**, page 115, to make 70 **triangle-square B's**. Repeat with remaining **rectangles** to make a total of 420 **triangle-square B's**, 70 from each color combination. (You will need 1 set of 4 matching **triangle-square B's** for *each* of the 99 blocks needed for the quilt.)

triangle-square B (make 70 of each)

3. Sew 1 **small square** and 1 **triangle-square A** together to make **Unit 1**. Make 4 **Unit 1's**.

Unit 1 (make 4)

4. Sew 4 matching **triangle-square B's** together to make 1 **Unit 2**.

Unit 2 (make 1)

5. Sew 2 **Unit 1's** and **Unit 2** together to make 1 **Unit 3**.

Unit 3 (make 1)

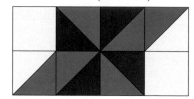

6. Sew 2 **small squares** and 1 **Unit 1** together to make **Unit 4**. Make 2 **Unit 4's**.

Unit 4 (make 2)

7. Sew 2 **Unit 4's** and **Unit 3** together to make 1 **Block**.

Block

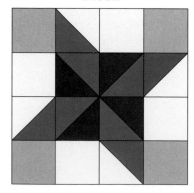

8. Repeat Steps 3 - 7 to make a total of 99 **Blocks**.
9. Referring to **Quilt Top Diagram**, page 19, sew **Blocks** together into rows. Sew rows together to make center section of quilt top.
10. Follow **Adding Squared Borders**, page 117, to sew **side**, then **top** and **bottom inner borders** to center section.
11. Sew 1 **border square** and 2 **border triangles** together to make **Border Unit**. Make 114 **Border Units**.

Border Unit (make 114)

12. Sew 1 **border square** and 2 **border triangles** together to make **Corner Border Unit**. Make 4 **Corner Border Units**.

Corner Border Unit (make 4)

13. In random color order, sew 26 **Border Units** and 1 **Corner Border Unit** together to make **Top/Bottom Pieced Border**. Make 2 **Top/Bottom Pieced Borders**.

Top/Bottom Pieced Border (make 2)

14. Sew 31 **Border Units** and 1 **Corner Border Unit** together to make **Side Pieced Border**. Make 2 **Side Pieced Borders**.

Side Pieced Border (make 2)

15. Follow Steps 1 - 3 of **Adding Mitered Borders**, page 118, to sew **Pieced Borders** to top, bottom, and sides of center section of quilt top.
16. To complete stitching at corners, fold 1 corner of quilt top diagonally with right sides together, matching outer edges of **Pieced Borders** as shown in **Fig. 2**. Beginning at point where previous seams end, sew borders together, backstitching at beginning and end of seam.

Fig. 2

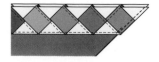

17. Repeat Step 16 to sew remaining **Pieced Border** corners together.
18. Follow **Adding Squared Borders**, page 117, to sew **side**, then **top** and **bottom outer borders** to center section to complete **Quilt Top**.

COMPLETING THE QUILT

1. Follow **Quilting**, page 118, to mark, layer, and quilt using **Quilting Diagram** as a suggestion. Our quilt is hand quilted.
2. Cut a 33" square of binding fabric. Follow **Binding**, page 122, to bind quilt using 2 1/2"w bias binding with mitered corners.

Quilting Diagram

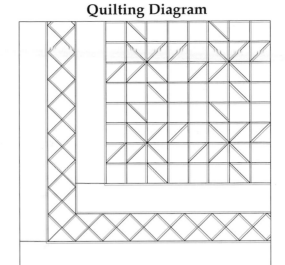

Quilt Top Diagram

19

CLAY'S CHOICE WALL HANGING

SKILL LEVEL: 1 2 3 4 5
BLOCK SIZE: 8" x 8"
WALL HANGING SIZE: 49" x 49"

YARDAGE REQUIREMENTS
Yardage is based on 45"w fabric.

- 1⅞ yds black print
- 1⅜ yds of cream solid
- ⅜ yd of yellow print
- 1 fat quarter (18" x 22" piece) *each* of 2 red, 2 blue, and 2 green prints
  3 yds for backing and hanging sleeve
  ¾ yd for binding
  52" x 52" batting

CUTTING OUT THE PIECES
All measurements include a ¼" seam allowance. Follow Rotary Cutting, page 112, to cut fabric.

1. **From black print:**
   - Cut 1 strip 10"w. From this strip, cut 6 **rectangles** 7" x 10" for triangle-square B's.
   - Cut 2 lengthwise **side outer borders** 3½" x 48½".
   - Cut 2 lengthwise **top/bottom outer borders** 3½" x 42½".
   - Cut 2 lengthwise **side inner borders** 2½" x 36½".
   - Cut 2 lengthwise **top/bottom inner borders** 2½" x 32½".
   - Cut 1 **large rectangle** 16" x 22" for triangle-square A's.

2. **From cream solid:** ▢
   - Cut 4 strips 2½"w. From these strips, cut 64 **small squares** 2½" x 2½".
   - Cut 3 strips 4½"w. From these strips, cut 26 squares 4½" x 4½". Cut squares twice diagonally to make 104 **border triangles**.
   - Cut 1 **large rectangle** 16" x 22" for triangle-square A's.

3. **From yellow print:** ▨
   - Cut 4 strips 2½"w. From these strips, cut 64 **small squares** 2½" x 2½".

4. **From red, blue, and green prints:** ◣
   - Cut 1 **rectangle** 7" x 10" from *each* fabric for triangle-square B's.
   - Cut 2 strips 2⅝" x 18" from *each* fabric. From these strips, cut a total of 52 **border squares** 2⅝" x 2⅝"

ASSEMBLING THE WALL HANGING TOP
Follow Piecing and Pressing, page 114, to make wall hanging top.

1. Using **large rectangles**, follow Step 1 of **Assembling the Quilt Top**, page 17, to make 70 **triangle-square A's.** (You will need 64 and have 6 left over.)

triangle-square A (make 70)

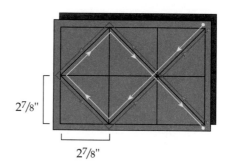

2. To make triangle-square B's, place 1 red and 1 black **rectangle** right sides together. Referring to **Fig. 1**, follow **Making Triangle-Squares**, page 115, to make 12 **triangle-square B's**. Repeat with remaining **rectangles** to make a total of 72 **triangle-square B's**, 12 from each color combination. (You will need 1 set of 4 matching **triangle-square B's** for *each* of the 16 blocks needed for the wall hanging.)

Fig. 1

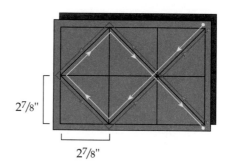

2⅞"

2⅞"

triangle-square B (make 12 of each)

3. Follow Steps 3 - 7 of **Assembling the Quilt Top**, page 18, to make a total of 16 **Blocks**.
4. Referring to **Wall Hanging Top Diagram**, sew **Blocks** together into rows. Sew rows together to make center section of wall hanging top.
5. Sew **top**, **bottom**, then **side inner borders** to center section.
6. Follow Step 11 of **Assembling the Quilt Top**, page 18, to make 48 **Border Units**.
7. Follow Step 12 of **Assembling the Quilt Top**, page 18, to make 4 **Corner Border Units**.
8. In random color order, sew 12 **Border Units** and 1 **Corner Border Unit** together to make **Pieced Border**. Make 4 **Pieced Borders**.

Pieced Border (make 4)

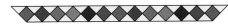

9. Follow Steps 15 - 17 of **Assembling the Quilt Top**, page 18, to sew **Pieced Borders** to center section.
10. Sew **top**, **bottom**, then **side outer borders** to center section to complete **Wall Hanging Top**.

COMPLETING THE WALL HANGING

1. Follow **Quilting**, page 118, to mark, layer, and quilt wall hanging using **Quilting Diagram**, page 19, as a suggestion. Our wall hanging is hand quilted.
2. Follow **Making a Hanging Sleeve**, page 124, to attach hanging sleeve to wall hanging.
3. Cut a 24" square of binding fabric. Follow **Binding**, page 122, to bind wall hanging using 2¹/₂"w bias binding with mitered corners.

Wall Hanging Top Diagram

pine-apple quilt

this cheerful quilt offers guests a warm welcome out of the cold. Named for the symbol of hospitality that it resembles, the Pineapple pattern was a favorite of pioneer women. To help you re-create this vintage spread in a lot less time, we've simplified the construction using paper foundation piecing — a classic technique that has found a new following! The design is drawn onto tracing paper and then "punched" using an unthreaded sewing machine. This creates a perforated pattern for precise piecing and alignment of fabric strips as they're sewn together. We also added corner triangles to the octagon-shaped pieces to form square blocks for faster assembly of the rows and to eliminate set-in squares.

PINEAPPLE QUILT

SKILL LEVEL: 1 2 3 4 5
BLOCK SIZE: 15" x 15"
QUILT SIZE: 76" x 91"

Our antique quilt uses cream set-in squares to join the octagonal pineapple blocks. We simplified the construction of this quilt by adding corner triangles to make each block square. This eliminates the set-in squares and makes assembly of the quilt top much easier.

YARDAGE REQUIREMENTS

Yardage is based on 45"w fabric. Yardages given for quilt top fabrics are approximate.

- ☐ 7 yds of cream solid
- ■ 3⅝ yds of red solid
- ■ 3⅜ yds of green solid
  5½ yds for backing
  ⅞ yd for binding
  90" x 108" batting

You will also need:
tracing paper (available at office supply stores in 19" x 24" tablets)

CUTTING OUT THE PIECES

*Follow **Rotary Cutting**, page 112, to cut fabric. Due to variations in individual work and the nature of paper piecing, the actual number of strips needed may vary.*

1. **From cream solid:** ☐
   - Cut 90 **strips** 1¾"w.
   - Cut 10 strips 7"w. From these strips, cut 60 squares 7" x 7". Cut squares once diagonally to make 120 **corner triangles**.

2. **From red solid:** ■
   - Cut 60 **strips** 1¾"w.
   - Cut 2 strips 2⅝"w. From these strips, cut 30 **center squares** 2⅝" x 2⅝".

3. **From green solid:** ■
   - Cut 60 **strips** 1¾"w.

MAKING THE PAPER FOUNDATIONS

1. To make a full-size foundation pattern from pattern, page 27, use a ruler to draw a line down the center of a piece of tracing paper. Turn paper 90° and draw a second line down the center perpendicular to the first line. Place paper over pattern, matching grey lines of pattern to intersecting lines on paper. Trace pattern. Turn paper and trace pattern in each remaining corner. Do not cut out.

2. To make foundations, stack up to 12 sheets of paper together and pin pattern on top, being careful not to pin over traced lines. Use an unthreaded sewing machine with stitch length set at approximately 8 stitches per inch to "sew" over traced lines of pattern, perforating the paper through all layers. These perforated lines will be your sewing lines. Trim foundations to approximately ¼" from outer line. Refer to **Block Diagram** and transfer corresponding numbers to each foundation. Repeat to make a total of 30 **foundations**.

ASSEMBLING THE QUILT TOP

1. (*Note:* Refer to **Block Diagram** for color placement. Numbers are not shown on **Figs. 1 - 4**.) Place 1 **center square** right side up over center square area on numbered side of 1 **foundation**; pin in place (**Fig. 1**). Hold foundation up to a light to make sure enough fabric extends beyond the center square outline (sewing line) for seam allowance.

Fig. 1

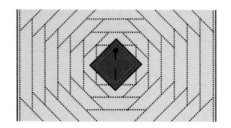

2. To cover area 1 on foundation, refer to **Fig. 2** to place 1 cream **strip** wrong side up on **center square**. Turn foundation over to paper side and sew directly on top of sewing line between center square and area 1, extending stitching a few stitches beyond beginning and end of line. Turn over to fabric side (**Fig. 2**).

Fig. 2

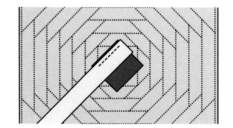

24

3. Trim strip even with ends of stitching. Trim seam allowance to a scant 1/4" if necessary (**Fig. 3**). Open out strip and trim off corners, making sure enough fabric extends beyond adjacent seamlines for seam allowance. Press and pin strip to foundation.

Fig. 3

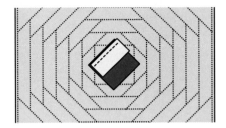

4. Repeat Steps 2 and 3 for areas 2, 3, and 4 (**Fig. 4**).

Fig. 4

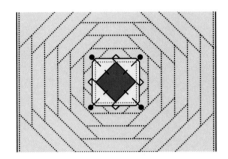

5. Referring to **Block Diagram**, repeat Steps 2 and 3 to add **strips** for areas 5 - 48 and to add **corner triangles** for areas 49 - 52 in numerical order. Trim block 1/4" from outer line of block outline on **foundation** to complete **Block**. Make 30 **Blocks**.

Block (make 30)

6. Sew 5 **Blocks** together to make **Row**. Make 6 **Rows**.

Row (make 6)

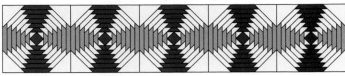

7. Referring to **Quilt Top Diagram**, page 26, sew **Rows** together. Carefully tear away **foundations** to complete **Quilt Top**.

COMPLETING THE QUILT

1. Follow **Quilting**, page 118, to mark, layer, and quilt using **Quilting Diagram** as a suggestion. Our quilt is hand quilted.
2. Cut a 30" square of binding fabric. Follow **Binding**, page 122, to bind quilt using 2 1/2"w bias binding with mitered corners.

Block Diagram

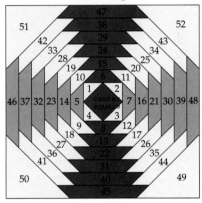

Quilting Diagram

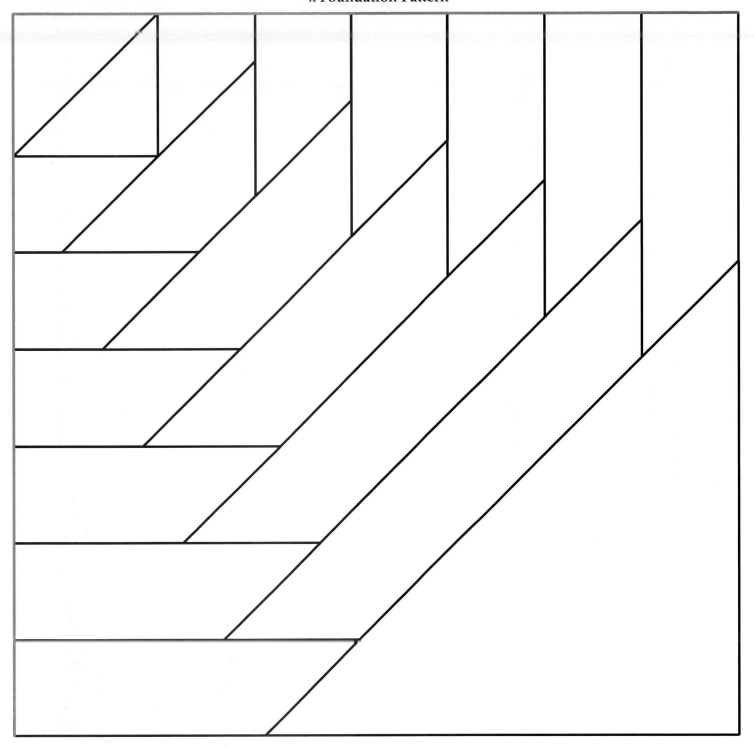

tree of life

the seasonal colors chosen for this quilt make it a wintertime favorite. Adapted from the classic Pine Tree design, the Tree of Life is one of America's oldest patchwork patterns, dating back to early Colonial times. The design, like many of the day, received its name from Bible verses that referred to the tree found in Paradise. For our variation, we simplified the pattern by using plain setting triangles along the quilt's edge in place of the half blocks used in the antique model shown here. Making the blocks is fast and easy using grid-pieced triangle-squares, and solid edgings create an interesting contrast when set against basic sashing strips. Pair the quilt with our coordinating accessories for a collection that's blissful to create!

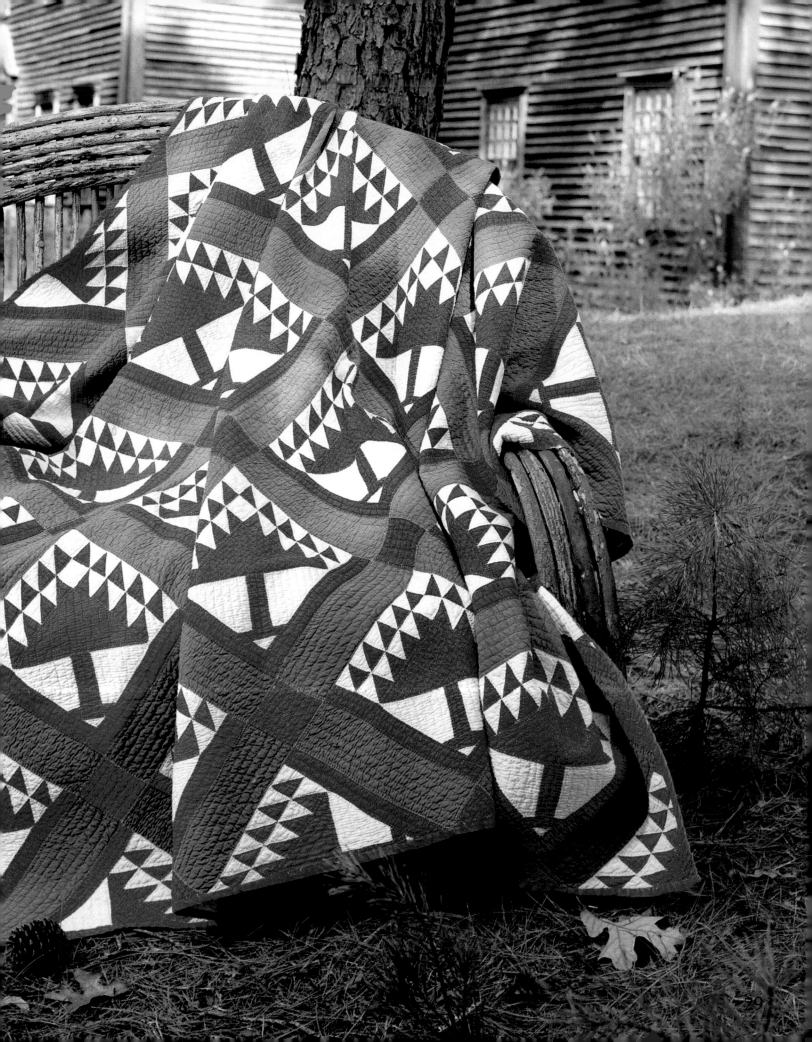

TREE OF LIFE QUILT

SKILL LEVEL: 1 2 3 4 5
BLOCK SIZE: 9^1/$_4$" x 9^1/$_4$"
QUILT SIZE: 69" x 86"

We simplified the piecing of this quilt by substituting solid setting triangles for the half blocks used on the edges of our antique quilt (see Assembly Diagram, page 34). We also resized the too-small quilt to fit a traditional twin-size bed.

YARDAGE REQUIREMENTS
Yardage is based on 45"w fabric.

■ 4³/₄ yds of red solid

□ 2⁵/₈ yds of cream solid

■ 2¹/₈ yds of green solid
  5¹/₄ yds for backing
  1 yd for binding
  81" x 96" batting

CUTTING OUT THE PIECES
All measurements include a ¼" seam allowance. Follow Rotary Cutting, page 112, to cut fabric.

1. **From red solid:** ■
   - Cut 2 strips 14³/₈"w. From these strips, cut 4 squares 14³/₈" x 14³/₈". Cut squares twice diagonally to make 16 **setting triangles** (you will need 14 and have 2 left over).
   - Cut 3 strips 3¹/₄"w. From these strips, cut 31 **sashing squares** 3¹/₄" x 3¹/₄".
   - Cut 16 strips 1¹/₂"w. From these strips, cut 32 **short inner borders** 1¹/₂" x 8³/₄" and 32 **long inner borders** 1¹/₂" x 9³/₄".
   - Cut 4 strips 1¹/₂"w. From these strips, cut 32 **trunks** 1¹/₂" x 4¹/₂".
   - Cut 1 strip 5¹/₈"w. From this strip, cut 5 squares 5¹/₈" x 5¹/₈". Cut squares twice diagonally to make 20 **sashing triangles** (you will need 18 and have 2 left over).
   - Cut 3 strips 6³/₈"w. From these strips, cut 16 squares 6³/₈" x 6³/₈". Cut squares once diagonally to make 32 **triangles**.
   - Cut 2 strips 2"w. From these strips, cut 32 **squares** 2" x 2".
   - Cut 6 **rectangles** 15" x 20" for triangle-squares.
   - Cut 2 squares 7³/₈" x 7³/₈". Cut squares once diagonally to make 4 **corner setting triangles**.

2. **From cream solid:** □
   - Cut 3 strips 1⁷/₈"w. From these strips, cut 64 **squares** 1⁷/₈" x 1⁷/₈".
   - Cut 1 strip 1¹/₄"w. From this strip, cut 32 **small squares** 1¹/₄" x 1¹/₄".
   - Cut 3 strips 6"w. From these strips, cut 16 squares 6" x 6". Cut squares twice diagonally to make 64 **triangles**.
   - Cut 6 **rectangles** 15" x 20" for triangle-squares.

3. **From green solid:** ■
   - Cut 20 strips 3¹/₄"w. From these strips, cut 80 **sashing strips** 3¹/₄"x 9³/₄".

ASSEMBLING THE QUILT TOP
Follow Piecing and Pressing, page 114, to make quilt top.

1. To make triangle-squares, place 1 red and 1 cream **rectangle** right sides together. Referring to **Fig. 1**, follow **Making Triangle-Squares**, page 115, to complete 96 **triangle-squares**. Repeat with remaining **rectangles** to make a total of 576 **triangle-squares**.

Fig. 1

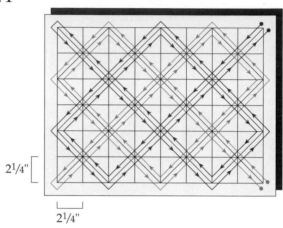

2¹/₄"
2¹/₄"

triangle-square (make 576)

2. Sew 10 **triangle-squares** and 2 **squares** together to make **Unit 1**. Make 32 **Unit 1's**.

Unit 1 (make 32)

3. Sew 8 **triangle-squares** together to make **Unit 2**. Make 32 **Unit 2's**.

Unit 2 (make 32)

4. Sew 1 **triangle**, 1 **Unit 2**, and 1 **Unit 1** together to make **Unit 3**. Make 32 **Unit 3's**.

Unit 3 (make 32)

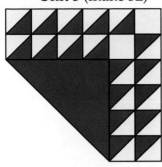

5. Referring to **Fig. 2**, sew 1 **trunk** and 2 **triangles** together. Trim trunk even with triangles to make **Unit 4**. Make 32 **Unit 4's**.

Fig. 2   **Unit 4** (make 32)

6. Place 1 **small square** and 1 **square** right sides together and matching edges. Sew diagonally across **small square** (**Fig. 3a**). Trim 1/4" beyond stitching (**Fig. 3b**) and press open to make **Unit 5**. Make 32 **Unit 5's**.

Fig. 3a   **Fig. 3b**

Unit 5 (make 32)

7. Place 1 **Unit 5** and 1 **Unit 4** right sides together and matching edges. Sew diagonally across **Unit 5** (**Fig. 4a**). Trim 1/4" beyond stitching (**Fig. 4b**) and press open to make **Unit 6**. Make 32 **Unit 6's**.

Fig. 4a   **Fig. 4b**

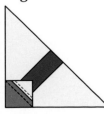 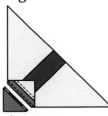

Unit 6 (make 32)

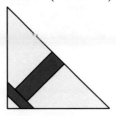

8. Sew 1 **Unit 3** and 1 **Unit 6** together to make **Unit 7**. Make 32 **Unit 7's.**

Unit 7 (make 32)

9. Sew **short**, then **long inner borders** to Unit 7 to complete **Block**. Make 32 **Blocks**.

Block (make 32)

10. Referring to **Assembly Diagram**, page 34, sew **corner setting triangles, sashing triangles, sashing strips, setting triangles, sashing squares,** and **Blocks** together into **Rows**. Sew **Rows** together to complete **Quilt Top**.

COMPLETING THE QUILT

1. Follow **Quilting**, page 118, to mark, layer, and quilt using **Quilting Diagram**, page 35, as a suggestion. Our quilt is hand quilted.
2. Cut a 30" square of binding fabric. Follow **Binding**, page 122, to bind quilt using 2¹/₂"w bias binding with mitered corners.

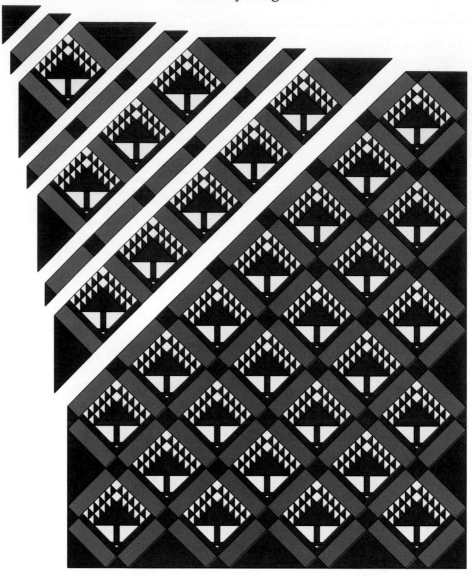

TREE OF LIFE PILLOW

PILLOW SIZE: 15" X 15"

YARDAGE REQUIREMENTS
Yardage is based on 45"w fabric.

- ³/₈ yd of red solid
- ³/₈ yd of cream print
- ¹/₈ yd of green print
  ¹/₂ yd for pillow top backing
  ¹/₂ yd for pillow back
  17" x 17" batting

You will also need:
  polyester fiberfill

CUTTING OUT THE PIECES
All measurements include a ¼" seam allowance. Follow
***Rotary Cutting**, page 112, to cut fabric.*

1. **From red solid:**
    - Cut 1 **large square** 8" x 8" for triangle-squares.
    - Cut 1 square 6³/₈" x 6³/₈". Cut square once diagonally to make 2 **triangles** (you will need 1 and have 1 left over).
    - Cut 4 **corner squares** 3¹/₂" x 3¹/₂".
    - Cut 1 **short inner border** 1¹/₂" x 8³/₄".
    - Cut 1 **long inner border** 1¹/₂" x 9³/₄".
    - Cut 1 **trunk** 1¹/₂" x 4¹/₂".
    - Cut 1 **square** 2" x 2".

2. **From cream print:**
- Cut 1 **large square** 8" x 8" for triangle-squares.
- Cut 2 **squares** 1⅞" x 1⅞".
- Cut 1 square 6" x 6". Cut square twice diagonally to make 2 **triangles** (you will need 2 and have 2 left over).
- Cut 1 **small square** 1¼" x 1¼".

3. **From green print:** ■
Cut 4 **outer borders** 3½" x 9¾".

ASSEMBLING THE PILLOW TOP
*Follow **Piecing and Pressing**, page, 114, to make pillow top.*

1. To make triangle-squares, place red and cream **large squares** right sides together. Referring to **Fig. 1**, follow **Making Triangle-Squares**, page 115, to complete 18 **triangle-squares**.

Fig. 1   **triangle-square** (make 18)

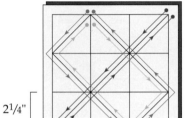

2¼"

2¼"

2. Follow Steps 2 - 9 of **Assembling the Quilt Top**, page 32, to make 1 **Block**.
3. Sew 1 **outer border** each to top and bottom of **Block**. Sew 1 **corner square** to each end of remaining **outer borders**; sew **outer borders** to sides of **Block** to complete **Pillow Top**.

COMPLETING THE PILLOW
1. Follow **Quilting**, page 118, to mark, layer, and quilt using **Quilting Diagram** as a suggestion. Our pillow top is hand quilted.
2. Follow **Making the Pillow**, page 124, to complete pillow.

Pillow Top Diagram

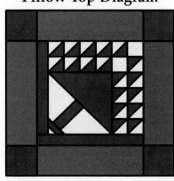

Quilting Diagram

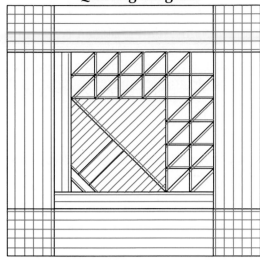

DELECTABLE MOUNTAINS TABLE QUILT

SKILL LEVEL: 1 2 3 4 5
BLOCK SIZE: 6¼" x 6¼"
QUILT SIZE: 25" x 32"

YARDAGE REQUIREMENTS
Yardage is based on 45"w fabric.

☐ 1⅛ yds of cream solid

■ 1 yd of red solid
⅞ yd for backing
¼ yd for binding
29" x 35" batting

CUTTING OUT THE PIECES
All measurements include a ¼" seam allowance. Follow Rotary Cutting, page 112, to cut fabric.

1. **From cream solid:** ☐
- Cut 2 strips 7½"w. From these strips, cut 10 squares 7½" x 7½". Cut squares twice diagonally to make 40 **triangles**.
- Cut 2 strips 1⅜"w. From these strips, cut 40 **squares** 1⅜" x 1⅜".
- Cut 2 **rectangles** 12" x 19" for triangle-squares.

2. **From red solid:** ■
- Cut 2 strips 5"w. From these strips, cut 10 squares 5" x 5". Cut squares twice diagonally to make 40 **medium triangles**.
- Cut 2 strips 1¾"w. From these strips, cut 40 squares 1¾" x 1¾". Cut squares once diagonally to make 80 **small triangles**.
- Cut 2 **rectangles** 12" x 19" for triangle-squares.

35

ASSEMBLING THE QUILT TOP

*Follow **Piecing and Pressing**, page 114, to make quilt top.*

1. To make triangle-squares, place 1 cream and 1 red **rectangle** right sides together. Referring to **Fig. 1**, follow **Making Triangle-Squares**, page 115, to complete 120 **triangle-squares**. Repeat with remaining rectangles to make a total of 240 **triangle-squares**.

Fig. 1

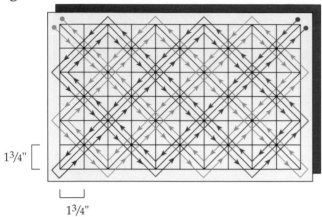

1³/₄"

1³/₄"

triangle-square (make 240)

2. Sew 3 **triangle-squares** and 1 **small triangle** together to make **Unit 1**. Make 40 **Unit 1's**. Sew 1 **square**, 3 **triangle-squares**, and 1 **small triangle** together to make **Unit 2**. Make 40 **Unit 2's**.

Unit 1 (make 40)

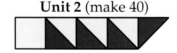

Unit 2 (make 40)

3. Sew 1 **Unit 1**, 1 **medium triangle**, and 1 **Unit 2** together to make **Unit 3**. Make 40 **Unit 3's**.

Unit 3 (make 40)

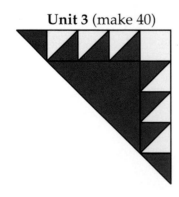

4. Sew 2 **Unit 3's** and 2 **triangles** together to make **Block**. Make 20 **Blocks**.

Block (make 20)

5. Sew 4 **Blocks** together to make **Row**. Make 5 **Rows**.

Row (make 5)

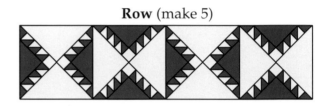

6. Referring to **Quilt Top Diagram**, sew **Rows** together to complete **Quilt Top**.

COMPLETING THE QUILT

1. Follow **Quilting**, page 118, to mark, layer, and quilt using **Quilting Diagram** as a suggestion. Our quilt is hand quilted.
2. Follow **Binding**, page 122, to bind quilt using 1³/₄"w straight-grain binding with mitered corners.

Quilt Top Diagram

Quilting Diagram

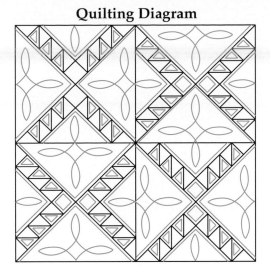

KANSAS TROUBLES PILLOW

BLOCK SIZE: 4³⁄₈" x 4³⁄₈"
PILLOW SIZE: 14" x 14" (including ruffle)

YARDAGE REQUIREMENTS

Yardage is based on 45"w fabric.

☐ ⅝ yd of cream print
■ ¼ yd of red solid
▨ ⅛ yd of green print
13" x 13" batting
⅜ yd for pillow top backing
⅜ yd for pillow back
1¼ yds of 1³⁄₄"w bias strip for welting
1¼ yds of ³⁄₁₆" cord for welting

You will also need:
polyester fiberfill

CUTTING OUT THE PIECES

All measurements include a ¼" seam allowance. Follow Rotary Cutting, page 112, to cut fabric.

1. **From cream print:**
   - Cut 1 **rectangle** 7" x 9" for triangle-squares.
   - Cut 2 squares 5¼" x 5¼". Cut squares once diagonally to make 4 **large triangles**.
   - Cut 4 **squares** 1³⁄₈" x 1³⁄₈".

2. **From red solid:**
   - Cut 1 **rectangle** 7" x 9" for triangle-squares.
   - Cut 2 squares 3½" x 3½". Cut squares once diagonally to make 4 **medium triangles**.
   - Cut 4 squares 1³⁄₄" x 1³⁄₄". Cut squares once diagonally to make 8 **small triangles**.

ASSEMBLING THE PILLOW TOP

Follow Piecing and Pressing, page 114, to make pillow top.

1. To make triangle-squares, place cream and red **rectangles** right sides together. Referring to **Fig. 1**, follow **Making Triangle-Squares**, page 115, to complete 24 **triangle-squares**.

Fig. 1

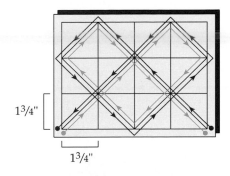

1³⁄₄"

1³⁄₄"

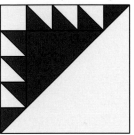

triangle-square (make 24)

2. Follow Steps 2 and 3 of **Assembling the Quilt Top**, page 36, to make 4 **Unit 3's** (you will need 4 **Unit 1's** and 4 **Unit 2's**).

3. Sew 1 **Unit 3** and 1 **large triangle** together to make **Block**. Make 4 **Blocks**.

Block (make 4)

4. Referring to photo, sew **Blocks** together to complete **Pillow Top**.

COMPLETING THE PILLOW

1. Follow **Quilting**, page 118, to mark, layer, and quilt using **Quilting Diagram**, this page, as a suggestion. Our pillow top is hand quilted.

2. Follow **Adding Welting**, page 124, to add welting.

3. For ruffle, cut 1 **strip** 3" x 91" from cream print and 1 **ruffle trim** 1¼" x 91" from green print, piecing as necessary. Matching long raw edges, sew right side of **ruffle trim** to wrong side of **strip**. Press 1 long edge of ruffle trim ¼" to wrong side. Fold pressed edge over to right side of strip, covering stitching line; topstitch in place. Sew short edges of ruffle together to form a large circle. Follow Steps 3-5 of **Adding a Ruffle**, page 125, to attach ruffle.

4. Follow **Making the Pillow**, page 124, to complete pillow.

endless stars

On a crisp, clear winter's night, the sky is brightened by an infinite array of twinkling stars. Those shimmering constellations no doubt inspired our Endless Stars pattern, which is traditionally known as Prairie Star. Although they appear to involve difficult angles, the stellar motifs of our quilt are quite simple to make — no templates are used at all! The angle markings on your rotary cutting ruler are the only guides you'll need to create perfect diamonds. Join them with basic triangles and large plain squares and watch the celestial show emerge. What a cozy way to "sleep under the stars!"

ENDLESS STARS QUILT

SKILL LEVEL: 1 2 3 4 5
QUILT SIZE: 73" x 82"

YARDAGE REQUIREMENTS

Yardage is based on 45"w fabric.

- 4 1/4 yds of cream solid
- 2 1/2 yds of brown print
- 3/4 yd of green print

5 yds for backing
1 yd for binding
81" x 96" batting

CUTTING OUT THE PIECES

All measurements include a 1/4" seam allowance. Follow ***Rotary Cutting****, page 112, to cut fabric.*

1. **From cream solid:**
   - Cut 8 **strips** 4 1/2"w.
   - Cut 2 lengthwise **side outer borders** 3 3/4" x 86".
   - Cut 2 lengthwise **top/bottom outer borders** 3 3/4" x 77".
   - From remaining fabric width, cut 7 strips 8 1/2"w. From these strips, cut 21 **large squares** 8 1/2" x 8 1/2".
   - Cut 4 squares 12 5/8" x 12 5/8". Cut squares twice diagonally to make 16 **side triangles**. (You will need 13 and have 3 left over.)
   - Cut 1 square 6 5/8" x 6 5/8". Cut square once diagonally to make 2 **corner triangles**.
2. **From brown print:**
   - Cut 2 lengthwise **side inner borders** 2 1/4" x 86".
   - Cut 2 lengthwise **top/bottom inner borders** 2 1/4" x 77".
   - From remaining fabric width, cut 12 strips 5 1/4"w. Place 2 strips right sides together. From pairs of strips, cut 56 pairs of rectangles 3" x 5 1/4". Referring to **Fig. 1**, cut each pair of rectangles once diagonally to make a total of 224 (112 in reverse) **right triangles**.

Fig. 1

right triangles (cut 224)

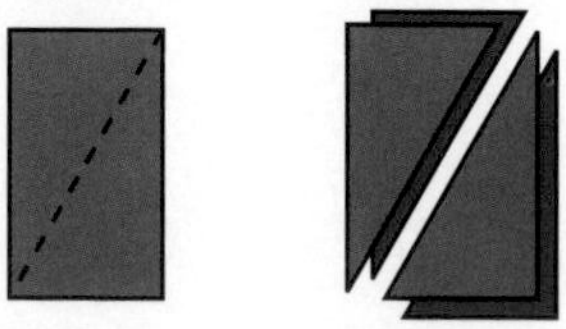

3. **From green print:**
   - Cut 3 strips 5 1/8"w. From these strips, cut 21 **squares** 5 1/8" x 5 1/8".
   - Cut 4 squares 7 7/8" x 7 7/8". Cut squares twice diagonally to make 16 **small side triangles**. (You will need 13 and have 3 left over.)
   - Cut 1 square 4 1/4" x 4 1/4". Cut square once diagonally to make 2 **small corner triangles**.

ASSEMBLING THE QUILT TOP

Follow ***Piecing and Pressing****, page 114, to make quilt top.*

1. Referring to **Fig. 2**, align 60° marking (shown in pink) on ruler with lower edge of 1 **strip**. Cut along right side of ruler to cut 1 end of strip at a 60° angle.

Fig. 2

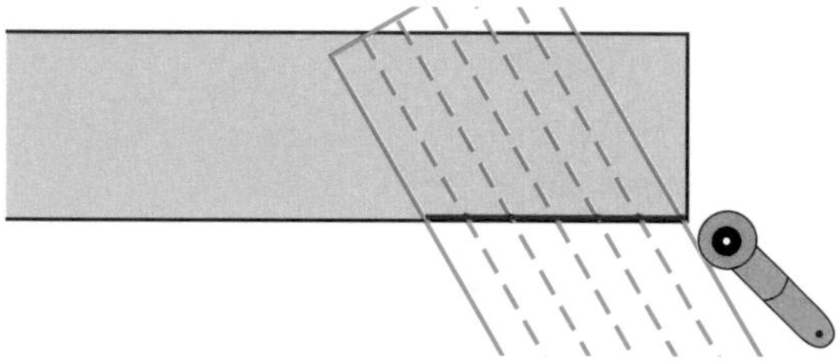

2. Turn cut **strip** 180° on mat and align 60° marking on ruler with lower edge of strip. Align previously cut 60° edge with 4 1/2" marking on ruler. Cut **strip** at 4 1/2" intervals as shown in **Fig. 3**.

Fig. 3

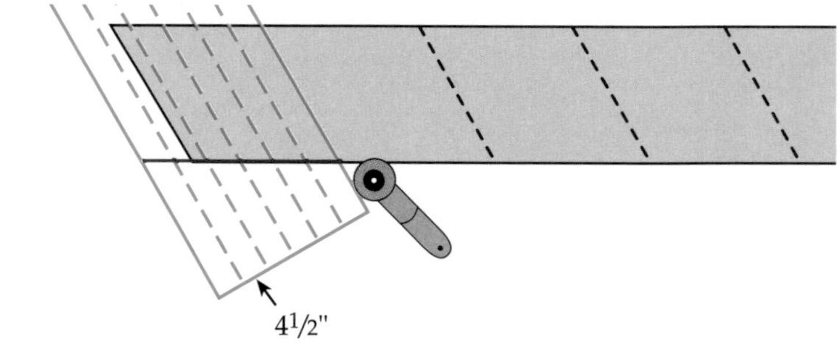

3. Repeat Steps 1 and 2 with remaining **strips** to cut a total of 56 **diamonds**.

diamond (cut 56)

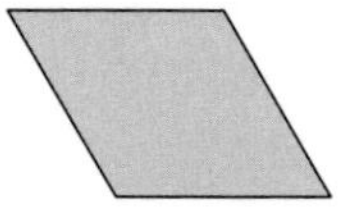

4. Sew 1 **diamond** and 4 **right triangles** together to make **Unit 1**. Make 56 **Unit 1's**.

Unit 1 (make 56)

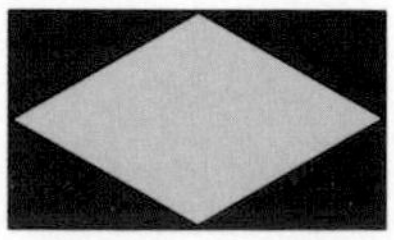

5. Referring to **Assembly Diagram**, sew **corner triangles**, **small side triangles**, **Unit 1's**, **squares**, **side triangles**, **large squares**, and **small corner triangles** together into diagonal rows. Sew rows together to make center section of quilt top.

6. Sew **side inner borders** and **side outer borders** together to make **Side Border Unit**. Make 2 **Side Border Units**. Sew **top/bottom inner borders** and **top/bottom outer borders** together to make **Top/Bottom Border Unit**. Make 2 **Top/Bottom Border Units**.

7. Referring to **Quilt Top Diagram**, follow **Adding Mitered Borders**, page 118, to sew **Border Units** to center section to complete **Quilt Top**.

COMPLETING THE QUILT

1. Follow **Quilting**, page 118, to mark, layer, and quilt, using **Quilting Diagram** as a suggestion. Our quilt is hand quilted.

2. Cut a 30" square of binding fabric. Follow **Binding**, page 122, to bind quilt using 2½"w bias binding with mitered corners.

Border Unit

Quilting Diagram

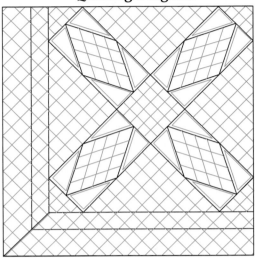

Assembly Diagram

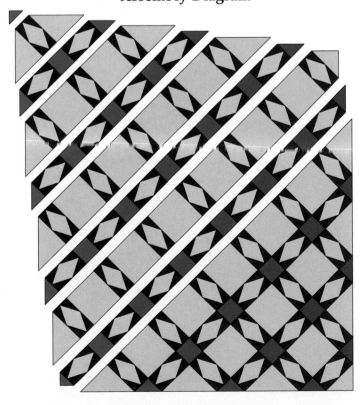

Quilt Top Diagram

41

castle in the mountains

The rustic colors of this classic cover-up will radiate warmth throughout the coldest winter months. Two old-time quilting favorites — the Castle Keep and Delectable Mountains patterns — combine with contemporary style for our handsome Castle in the Mountains quilt. The block-within-a-block look of the Castle Keep design is produced using grid-pieced units, along with rotary cut triangles and squares. The blocks are set together without sashing for an intriguing arrangement of geometric shapes. A range of Delectable Mountains motifs, made with simple templates, forms a majestic inner border. The soothing, muted shades of the blocks are echoed in the outer borders.

CASTLE IN THE MOUNTAINS QUILT

SKILL LEVEL: 1 2 3 4 5
BLOCK SIZE: 18" x 18"
QUILT SIZE: 79" x 97"

YARDAGE REQUIREMENTS
Yardage is based on 45"w fabric.

- 5¼ yds of burgundy print
- 3⅜ yds of navy solid
- 3 yds of tan solid
- 2¾ yds of plaid
- 1⅞ yds of tan print
- ½ yd of dark burgundy print
- 7¼ yds for backing
- 1 yd for binding
- 90" x 108" batting

CUTTING OUT THE PIECES
All measurements include a ¼" seam allowance. Follow Rotary Cutting, page 112, to cut fabric.

1. **From burgundy print:** ◼
   - Cut 5 strips 3⅞"w. From these strips, cut 48 squares 3⅞" x 3⅞". Cut squares once diagonally to make 96 **triangles**.
   - Cut 2 strips 1½"w. From these strips, cut 48 **small squares** 1½" x 1½".
   - Cut 1 strip 2½"w. From this strip, cut 12 **medium squares** 2½" x 2½".
   - Cut 16 strips 3½"w. From these strips, cut 192 **large squares** 3½" x 3½".
   - Cut 2 lengthwise **side outer borders** 4¾" x 92".
   - Cut 2 lengthwise **top/bottom outer borders** 4¾" x 82".

2. **From navy solid:** ◼
   - Cut 14 **strips** 2"w for pieced borders.
   - Cut 2 lengthwise **side inner borders** 1½" x 84".
   - Cut 2 lengthwise **top/bottom inner borders** 1½" x 68".
   - From remaining fabric width, cut 1 **large rectangle** 14" x 21" for large triangle-squares.
   - From remaining fabric width, cut 1 **small rectangle** 13" x 16" for small triangle-squares.

3. **From tan solid:** ◻
   - Cut 20 strips 3½"w. From these strips, cut 96 **rectangles** 3½" x 6½" and 48 **large squares** 3½" x 3½".
   - Cut 2 strips 1½"w. From these strips, cut 48 **small squares** 1½" x 1½".
   - Cut 1 **large rectangle** 14" x 21" for large triangle-squares.
   - Cut 1 **small rectangle** 13" x 16" for small triangle-squares.

4. **From plaid:** ◼
   - Cut 2 lengthwise **side middle borders** 3¼" x 86".
   - Cut 2 lengthwise **top/bottom middle borders** 3¼" x 74".

5. **From tan print:** ◼
   - Cut 14 **strips** 2"w for pieced borders.
   - Cut 4 strips 3½"w. From these strips, cut 48 **large squares** 3½" x 3½".
   - Cut 3 strips 4¼"w. From these strips, cut 24 squares 4¼" x 4¼". Cut squares twice diagonally to make 96 **small triangles**.
   - Cut 4 **corner squares** 4½" x 4½".

6. **From dark burgundy print:** ◼
   - Cut 3 strips 4¼"w. From these strips, cut 24 squares 4¼" x 4¼". Cut squares twice diagonally to make 96 **small triangles**.

ASSEMBLING THE QUILT TOP
Follow Piecing and Pressing, page 114, to make quilt top.

MAKING THE BLOCKS

1. To make small triangle-squares, place tan and navy **small rectangles** right sides together. Referring to **Fig. 1**, follow **Making Triangle-Squares**, page 115, to make 96 **small triangle-squares**.

Fig. 1

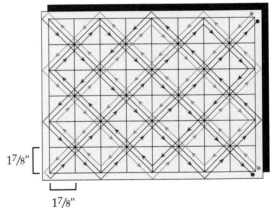

17⅞"
17⅞"

small triangle-square (make 96)

2. Sew 2 **small triangle-squares** and 2 **small squares** together to make **Unit 1**. Make 48 **Unit 1's**.

Unit 1 (make 48)

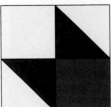

3. To make large triangle-squares, place tan and navy **large rectangles** right sides together. Referring to **Fig. 2,** follow **Making Triangle-Squares,** page 115, to make 48 **large triangle-squares**.

Fig. 2

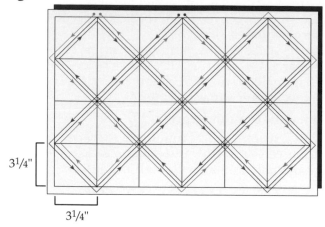

$3^1/4"$

$3^1/4"$

large triangle-square (make 48)

4. Referring to **Fig. 3,** place 2 **large triangle-squares** right sides and opposite colors together, matching seams. Referring to **Fig. 4,** draw a diagonal line (shown in pink) from corner to corner. Stitch ¼" on both sides of drawn line. Cut on drawn line and press open to make 2 **triangle units**. Repeat with remaining **large triangle-squares** to make a total of 48 **triangle units**.

Fig. 3   **Fig. 4**

triangle unit (make 48)

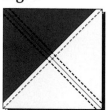

5. Sew 2 **Unit 1's** and 1 **triangle unit** together to make **Unit 2**. Make 24 **Unit 2's**.

Unit 2 (make 24)

6. Sew 2 **triangle units** and 1 **medium square** together to make **Unit 3**. Make 12 **Unit 3's**.

Unit 3 (make 12)

7. Sew 2 **Unit 2's** and 1 **Unit 3** together to make **Unit 4**. Make 12 **Unit 4's**.

Unit 4 (make 12)

8. Sew 2 **small triangles** together to make **Unit 5**. Make 48 **Unit 5's**. Sew 2 **small triangles** together to make **Unit 6**. Make 48 **Unit 6's**.

Unit 5 (make 48)   **Unit 6** (make 48)

9. Sew 1 **triangle** and 1 **Unit 5** together to make **Unit 7**. Make 48 **Unit 7's**. Sew 1 **triangle** and 1 **Unit 6** together to make **Unit 8**. Make 48 **Unit 8's**.

Unit 7 (make 48)   **Unit 8** (make 48)

10. Sew 1 **Unit 7** and 1 **Unit 8** together to make **Unit 9**. Make 48 **Unit 9's**.

Unit 9 (make 48)

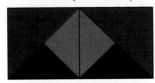

11. Sew 2 **large squares** and 1 **Unit 9** together to make **Unit 10**. Make 24 **Unit 10's**.

Unit 10 (make 24)

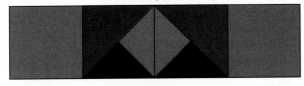

12. Sew 2 **Unit 9's**, 1 **Unit 4**, then 2 **Unit 10's** together to make **Unit 11**. Make 12 **Unit 11's**.

Unit 11 (make 12)

13. Place 1 **large square** on 1 **rectangle** with right sides together and stitch diagonally (**Fig. 5**). Trim 1/4" from stitching line (**Fig. 6**). Press open, pressing seam allowance toward darker fabric.

Fig. 5   **Fig. 6**

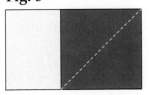

14. Place 1 **large square** on opposite end of **rectangle** and stitch diagonally (**Fig. 7**). Trim and press open as in Step 13 to make **Unit 12**.

Fig. 7   **Unit 12**

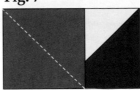   

15. Repeat Steps 13 and 14 to make a total of 96 **Unit 12's**.
16. Sew 2 **Unit 12's** together to make **Unit 13**. Make 48 **Unit 13's**.

Unit 13 (make 48)

17. Sew 2 **large squares** and 1 **Unit 13** together to make **Unit 14**. Make 24 **Unit 14's**.

Unit 14 (make 24)

18. Sew 2 **Unit 13's**, 1 **Unit 11**, then 2 **Unit 14's** together to make **Block**. Make 12 **Blocks**.

Block (make 12)

19. Sew 3 **Blocks** together to make **Row**, page 48. Make 4 **Rows**.

Row (make 4)

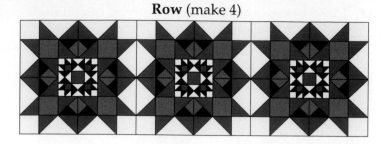

20. Referring to **Quilt Top Diagram**, sew **Rows** together to make center section of quilt top.

MAKING THE PIECED BORDER

1. Follow Step 1 of **Template Cutting**, page 114, and use patterns, page 51, to make **Templates A**, **B**, and **C**.
2. Place 2 tan **strips** right sides together. Referring to **Fig. 8**, use **Template A** to mark 28 **A's** on top **strip**. Keeping **strips** stacked together, use rotary cutter and ruler to cut 28 pairs of **A's**. (You will cut 28 **A's** and 28 **reverse A's** from strips). Repeat using navy **strips**.

Fig. 8

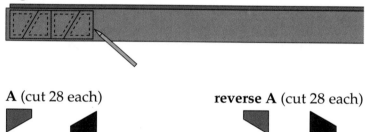

A (cut 28 each)   **reverse A** (cut 28 each)

3. Referring to Step 2, use 3 pairs of tan **strips** and **Template B** to cut a total of 28 **B's** and 28 **reverse B's**. Repeat using navy **strips**.

B (cut 28 each)   **reverse B** (cut 28 each)

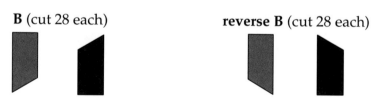

4. Referring to Step 2, use 2 pairs of tan **strips** and **Template C** to cut a total of 28 **C's** and 28 **reverse C's**. Repeat using navy **strips**.

C (cut 28 each)   **reverse C** (cut 28 each)

5. Referring to diagrams for color placement, use 1 **A** (tan) and 1 **B** (navy) to make **Unit 15**; use 2 **C's** to make **Unit 16**; use 1 **A** (navy) and 1 **B** (tan) to make **Unit 17**; use 1 **reverse A** (navy) and 1 **reverse B** (tan) to make **Unit 18**; use 2 **reverse C's** to make **Unit 19**; and use 1 **reverse A** (tan) and 1 **reverse B** (navy) to make **Unit 20**. Make 28 each of **Units 15 - 20**.

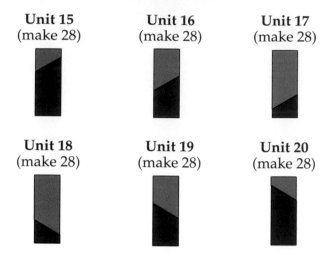

Unit 15 (make 28)   Unit 16 (make 28)   Unit 17 (make 28)

Unit 18 (make 28)   Unit 19 (make 28)   Unit 20 (make 28)

6. Sew 1 each of **Unit 15**, **Unit 16**, **Unit 17**, **Unit 18**, **Unit 19**, and **Unit 20** together to make **Border Unit**. Make 28 **Border Units**.

Border Unit (make 28)

7. Sew 8 **Border Units** together to make **Side Pieced Border**. Make 2 **Side Pieced Borders**.

Side Pieced Border (make 2)

8. Sew 2 **corner squares** and 6 **Border Units** together to make **Top/Bottom Pieced Border**. Make 2 **Top/Bottom Pieced Borders**.

Top/Bottom Pieced Border (make 2)

9. Sew **Side**, then **Top** and **Bottom Pieced Borders** to center section of quilt top.
10. Referring to **Quilt Top Diagram**, follow **Adding Squared Borders**, page 117, to add **side**, then **top** and **bottom inner borders**. Repeat to add **middle** and **outer borders** to complete **Quilt Top**.

COMPLETING THE QUILT

1. Follow **Quilting**, page 118, to mark, layer, and quilt using **Quilting Diagram** as a suggestion. Our quilt is hand quilted.
2. Cut a 32" square of binding fabric. Follow **Binding**, page 122, to bind quilt using 2¹/₂"w bias binding with mitered corners.

Quilting Diagram

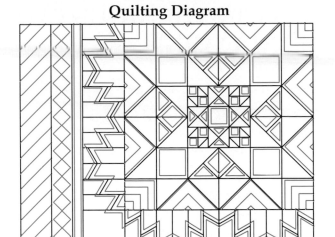

Quilt Top Diagram

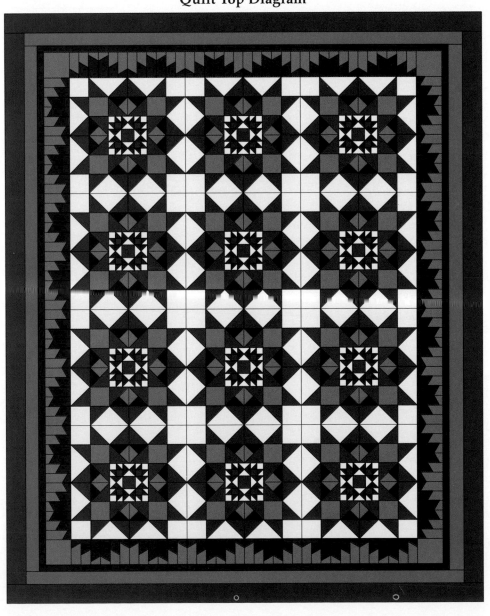

CASTLE IN THE MOUNTAINS WALL HANGING

SKILL LEVEL: 1 2 3 4 5
WALL HANGING SIZE: 39" x 39"

YARDAGE REQUIREMENTS

Yardage is based on 45"w fabric.

- 7/8 yd of burgundy print
- 5/8 yd of navy solid
- 1/2 yd of tan print
- 3/8 yd of plaid
- 1/4 yd of burgundy solid
- 1/2 yd of tan solid
  1 5/8 yds for backing and hanging sleeve
  3/8 yd for binding
  42" x 42" batting

CUTTING OUT THE PIECES

All measurements include a 1/4" seam allowance. Follow Rotary Cutting, page 112, to cut fabric.

1. **From burgundy print:** ■
   - Cut 4 strips 3 3/8"w for **outer borders**.
   - Cut 2 strips 3 1/2"w. From these strips, cut 16 **large squares** 3 1/2" x 3 1/2".
   - Cut 4 squares 3 7/8" x 3 7/8". Cut squares once diagonally to make 8 **triangles**.
   - Cut 4 **small squares** 1 1/2" x 1 1/2".
   - Cut 1 **medium square** 2 1/2" x 2 1/2".

2. **From navy solid:** ■
   - Cut 4 **strips** 2"w for pieced borders.
   - Cut 4 strips 1 1/2"w for **inner borders**.
   - Cut 1 **square** 5" x 5" for small triangle-squares.
   - Cut 1 **large rectangle** 5" x 8" for large triangle-squares.

3. **From tan print:** ■
   - Cut 4 **strips** 2"w for pieced borders.
   - Cut 4 **corner squares** 4 1/2" x 4 1/2".
   - Cut 4 **large squares** 3 1/2" x 3 1/2".
   - Cut 2 squares 4 1/4" x 4 1/4". Cut squares twice diagonally to make 8 **small triangles**.

4. **From plaid:** ■
   - Cut 4 strips 2 1/2"w for **middle borders**.

5. **From burgundy solid:** ■
   - Cut 2 squares 4 1/4" x 4 1/4". Cut squares twice diagonally to make 8 **small triangles**.

6. **From tan solid:** ▢
   - Cut 2 strips 3 1/2"w. From these strips, cut 8 **rectangles** 3 1/2" x 6 1/2" and 4 **large squares** 3 1/2" x 3 1/2".
   - Cut 1 **large rectangle** 5" x 8" for large triangle-squares.

- Cut 4 **small squares** 1 1/2" x 1 1/2".
- Cut 1 **square** 5" x 5" for small triangle-squares.

ASSEMBLING THE WALL HANGING TOP

Follow Piecing and Pressing, page 114, to make wall hanging top.

1. To make small triangle-squares, place tan and navy **squares** right sides together. Referring to **Fig. 1**, follow **Making Triangle-Squares**, page 115, to make 8 **small triangle-squares**.

Fig. 1

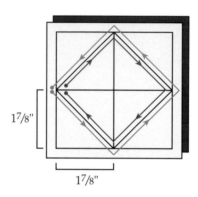

1 7/8"   1 7/8"

small triangle-square (make 8)

2. Sew 2 **small triangle-squares** and 2 **small squares** together to make **Unit 1**. Make 4 **Unit 1's**.

Unit 1 (make 4)

3. To make large triangle-squares, place tan and navy **large rectangles** right sides together. Referring to **Fig. 2**, follow **Making Triangle-Squares**, page 115, to make 4 **large triangle-squares**.

Fig. 2

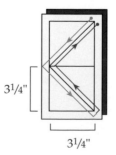

3 1/4"   3 1/4"

50

large triangle-square (make 4)

4. Referring to Step 4 of **Assembling the Quilt Top**, page 46, use **large triangle-squares** to make a total of 4 **triangle units**.

5. Referring to Steps 5 - 12 of **Assembling the Quilt Top**, page 46, make 1 **Unit 11**. (You will need 2 **Unit 2's**, 1 **Unit 3**, 1 **Unit 4**, 4 **Unit 5's**, 4 **Unit 6's**, 4 **Unit 7's**, 4 **Unit 8's**, 4 **Unit 9's**, and 2 **Unit 10's**.)

6. Refer to Steps 13 - 18 of **Assembling the Quilt Top**, page 47, to make 1 **Block**. (You will need 1 **Unit 11**, 8 **Unit 12's**, 4 **Unit 13's**, and 2 **Unit 14's**.)

7. Follow Step 1 of **Making the Pieced Border**, page 48, to make **Templates**.

8. Fold 1 tan **strip** in half with right sides together. Referring to Step 2 of **Making the Pieced Border**, page 48, mark and cut 8 **A's** and 8 **reverse A's** from folded strip. Repeat using navy **strip**.

9. Using 2 tan strips, refer to Step 3 of **Making the Pieced Border**, page 48, to cut 8 **B's** and 8 **reverse B's**. Repeat using navy **strips**.

10. Fold remaining tan **strip** in half with right sides together. Referring to Step 4 of **Making the Pieced Border**, page 48, cut 8 **C's** and 8 **reverse C's.** Repeat using navy **strip**.

11. Referring to Steps 5 and 6 of **Making the Pieced Border**, page 48, make 8 **Border Units**. (You will need 8 each of **Units 15 - 20**.)

12. Sew 2 **Border Units** together to make **Pieced Border**. Make 4 **Pieced Borders**.

Pieced Border (make 4)

13. Referring to **Wall Hanging Top Diagram**, sew 1 **Pieced Border** each to top and bottom edges of **Block**. Sew 1 **corner square** to each end of each remaining **Pieced Border**; sew borders to side edges of **Block** to make center section of wall hanging top.

14. Follow **Adding Squared Borders**, page 117, to sew **top**, **bottom**, then **side inner borders** to center section. Repeat to add **middle** and **outer borders** to complete **Wall Hanging Top**.

COMPLETING THE WALL HANGING

1. Follow **Quilting**, page 118, to mark, layer, and quilt using **Quilting Diagram**, page 49, as a suggestion. Our wall hanging is hand quilted.

2. Follow **Making a Hanging Sleeve**, page 124, to attach hanging sleeve to wall hanging back.

3. Follow **Binding**, page 122, to bind wall hanging using 2¹/₂"w straight-grain binding with overlapped corners.

Wall Hanging Top Diagram

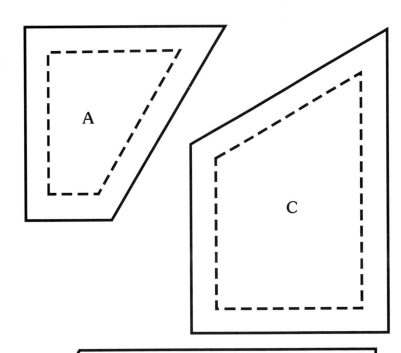

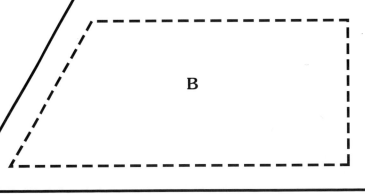

jacob's ladder

Winter is an ideal time to curl up in a warm blanket and read a good book. Stories from the Bible provided a wealth of inspiration for early quilters. This influence is reflected in the titles of many classic patterns we love today. One such design, known as Jacob's Ladder, was named for the vision in which God revealed his covenant with the children of Israel. Arranged in a straight-furrows setting, the contrasting squares of our quilt represent the angel-trod steps from heaven that appeared in Jacob's dream. The design is simple to create using easy grid-pieced triangle-squares and strip-set units. A plain outer border finishes the quilt with a divinely soft edge.

JACOB'S LADDER QUILT

SKILL LEVEL: 1 2 3 4 5
BLOCK SIZE: 12" x 12"
QUILT SIZE: 93" x 105"

YARDAGE REQUIREMENTS

Yardage is based on 45"w fabric.

- ■ 7¼ yds of brown print
- □ 5¾ yds of cream print
  8½ yds for backing
  1 yd for binding
  120" x 120" batting

CUTTING OUT THE PIECES

All measurements include a ¼" seam allowance. Follow
Rotary Cutting, page 112, to cut fabric.

1. **From brown print:**
    - Cut 43 **strips** 2"w.
    - Cut 2 lengthwise **side borders** 4½" x 112".
    - Cut 2 lengthwise **top/bottom borders** 4½" x 100".
    - Cut 9 **squares** 21" x 21" for triangle-squares.

2. **From cream print:** □
    - Cut 43 **strips** 2"w.
    - Cut 9 **squares** 21" x 21" for triangle-squares.

ASSEMBLING THE QUILT TOP

Follow Piecing and Pressing, page 114, to make quilt top.

1. Sew 2 **strips** together to make **Strip Set**. Make 43 **Strip Sets**. Cut across **Strip Sets** at 2" intervals to make 896 **Unit 1's**.

Strip Set (make 43)

2"

Unit 1 (cut 896)

2. Sew 2 **Unit 1's** together to make **Unit 2**. Make 448 **Unit 2's**.

Unit 2 (make 448)

3. To make **triangle-squares**, place 1 brown and 1 cream **square** right sides together. Referring to **Fig. 1**, follow **Making Triangle-Squares**, page 115, to make 50 **triangle-squares**. Repeat with remaining **squares** to make a total of 450 **triangle-squares**. (You will need 448 and have 2 left over.)

Fig. 1

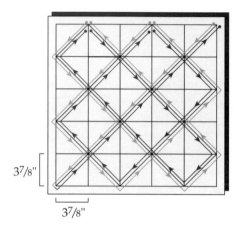

37/8"

37/8"

triangle-square (make 450)

4. Sew 2 **triangle-squares** and 2 **Unit 2's** together to make **Unit 3**. Make 112 **Unit 3's**.

Unit 3 (make 112)

5. Sew 2 **triangle-squares** and 2 **Unit 2's** together to make **Unit 4**. Make 112 **Unit 4's**.

Unit 4 (make 112)

6. Sew 2 **Unit 3's** and 2 **Unit 4's** together to make **Block**. Make 56 **Blocks**.

Block (make 56)

7. Sew 7 **Blocks** together to make **Row**. Make 8 **Rows**.

Row (make 8)

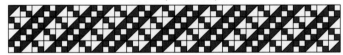

8. Referring to **Quilt Top Diagram**, sew **Rows** together to make center section of quilt top.
9. Follow **Adding Mitered Borders,** page 118, to add **borders** to center section to complete **Quilt Top**.

COMPLETING THE QUILT

1. Follow **Quilting**, page 118, to layer and quilt. Our quilt is quilted in the ditch by hand.
2. Cut a 34" square of binding fabric. Follow **Binding**, page 122, to bind quilt using 2½"w bias binding with mitered corners.

Quilt Top Diagram

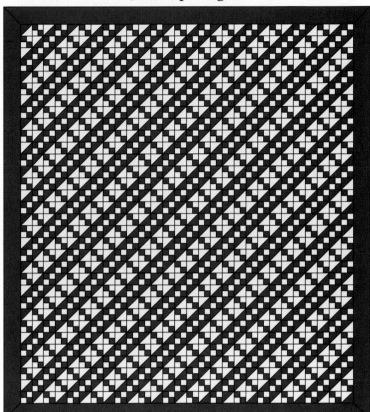

55

adirondack quilt

The Adirondack Mountains, far upstate from the bustle of New York City, has long been a popular winter retreat where simple pleasures are the greatest rewards. Our Adirondack Collection captures that spirit with an array of rustic designs. A handsome accent for the lodge, this Adirondack quilt is a variation of the Bear's Paw pattern. A variety of fabrics is used to create its complex-looking arrangement, but the pattern is actually a breeze to make using our grid-piecing method for the triangle-squares. The woodsy motifs featured on the pillow flip are quickly fused in place and machine appliquéd using clear nylon thread.

58

ADIRONDACK QUILT

SKILL LEVEL: 1 2 3 4 5
BLOCK SIZE: 12¼" x 12¼"
QUILT SIZE: 82" x 108"

YARDAGE REQUIREMENTS
Yardage is based on 45"w fabric.

- 4¼ yds of dark brown check
- 3½ yds of tan print
- 2¾ yds **total** of assorted plaids, stripes, and checks (our quilt uses 5 different fabrics)
- 2⅜ yds of red print
- 1¼ yds of dark red print
- ⅞ yd of green solid
- ⅜ yd of gold plaid
- 1 fat quarter (18" x 22" piece) **each** of green plaid and green print for tree appliqués
  7¾ yds for backing
  1 yd for binding
  120" x 120" batting

You will also need:
  paper-backed fusible web
  transparent monofilament thread for appliqué

CUTTING OUT THE PIECES
All measurements include a ¼" seam allowance. Follow Rotary Cutting, page 112, to cut fabric.

1. **From dark brown check:**
   - Cut 6 **strips** 5¾"w.
   - Cut 2 lengthwise strips 4" x 104" for **side outer borders**.
   - Cut 2 lengthwise strips 4" x 85" for **top/bottom outer borders**.
   - Cut 21 strips 2¼"w from fabric width remaining after cutting borders. From these strips, cut a total of 84 **rectangles** 2¼" x 5¾".

2. **From tan print:**
   - Cut 1 lengthwise strip 13¾" x 76" for **pillow flip**.
   - Cut 8 **large rectangles** 17" x 20" for triangle-squares.

3. **From assorted plaids, stripes, and checks:**
   - Cut 21 strips 4"w. From these strips, cut 168 **large squares** 4" x 4". (For each of the 42 blocks, you will need 4 matching **large squares**.)

4. **From red print:**
   - Cut 1 lengthwise strip 1¼" x 76" for **top inner border**.
   - Cut 4 **large rectangles** 17" x 20" for triangle-squares.

5. **From dark red print:**
   - Cut 4 **large rectangles** 17" x 20" for triangle-squares.

6. **From green solid:**
   - Cut 10 strips 2¼"w. From these strips, cut 168 **squares** 2¼" x 2¼".

7. **From gold plaid:**
   - Cut 3 **strips** 2¼"w.

PREPARING THE APPLIQUÉS
*Follow **Preparing Appliqué Pieces**, page 116, to cut pieces using patterns, pages 69 - 71.*

1. **From dark brown check:**
   - Cut 4 **Bears** (2 in reverse).

2. **From dark red print:**
   - Cut 5 **Small Tree Trunks**.
   - Cut 3 **Large Tree Trunks**.

3. **From green solid:**
   - Cut 2 **Tree A's**.

4. **From gold plaid:**
   - Cut 3 **Large Moons**.

5. **From green plaid:**
   - Cut 3 **Tree A's**.

6. **From green print:**
   - Cut 3 **Tree A's**.

ASSEMBLING THE QUILT TOP
*Follow **Piecing and Pressing**, page 114, to make quilt top.*

1. Assemble **strips** as shown to make **Strip Set**. Make 3 **Strip Sets**. Cut across **Strip Sets** at 2¼" intervals to make 42 **Unit 1's**.

Strip Set (make 3)   **Unit 1** (make 42)

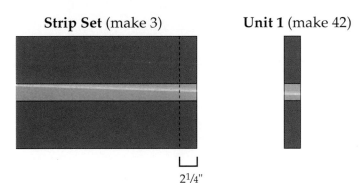

2¼"

2. To make triangle-square A's, place 1 tan print and 1 red print **large rectangle** right sides together. Referring to **Fig. 1**, follow Steps 1 - 3 of **Making Triangle-Squares**, page 115, to draw a grid of 42 squares $2^5/_8"$ x $2^5/_8"$. Referring to **Fig. 2** for stitching directions, follow Steps 4 - 6 of **Making Triangle-Squares** to make 84 **triangle-square A's**. Repeat to complete 336 **triangle-square A's**.

Fig. 1

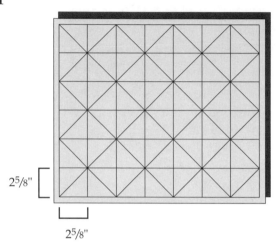

$2^5/_8"$

$2^5/_8"$

Fig. 2

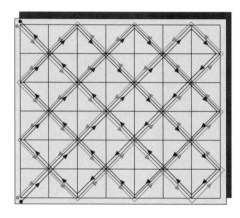

triangle-square A (make 336)

3. Using dark red print **large rectangles** and remaining tan print **large rectangles**, repeat Step 2 to make a total of 336 **triangle-square B's**.

triangle-square B (make 336)

4. Assemble 2 **triangle-square A's** to make **Unit 2**. Make 84 **Unit 2's**.

Unit 2 (make 84)

5. Assemble 2 **triangle-square A's** and 1 **square** to make **Unit 3**. Make 84 **Unit 3's**.

Unit 3 (make 84)

6. Assemble 1 **Unit 2**, 1 **large square**, and 1 **Unit 3** to make **Unit 4**. Make 84 **Unit 4's**.

Unit 4 (make 84)

7. Assemble 2 **Unit 4's** and 1 **rectangle** to make **Unit 5**. Make 42 **Unit 5's**.

Unit 5 (make 42)

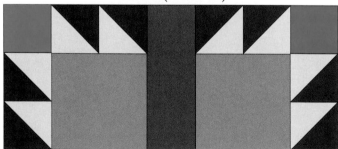

8. Assemble 1 **Unit 1** and 2 **Unit 5's** to make **Block A**. Make 21 **Block A's**.

Block A (make 21)

9. Use **triangle-square B's** and repeat Steps 4 - 8 to make 21 **Block B's**.

Block B (make 21)

10. Referring to **Quilt Top Diagram**, page 64, assemble **Blocks** into rows; sew rows together to make center section of quilt top.
11. Referring to **Quilt Top Diagram**, page 64, follow **Almost Invisible Appliqué**, page 116, to stitch appliqués to **pillow flip**.
12. Follow **Adding Squared Borders**, page 117, to attach **pillow flip**, then **top inner border** to center section of quilt top.
13. Follow **Adding Squared Borders**, page 117, to attach **side**, then **top** and **bottom outer borders** to complete **Quilt Top**.

COMPLETING THE QUILT

1. Follow **Quilting**, page 118, to mark, layer, and quilt, using **Quilting Diagram** as a suggestion. Our quilt is hand quilted.
2. Cut a 34" square of binding fabric. Follow **Binding**, page 122, to bind quilt using 2½"w bias binding with mitered corners.

Quilting Diagram

63

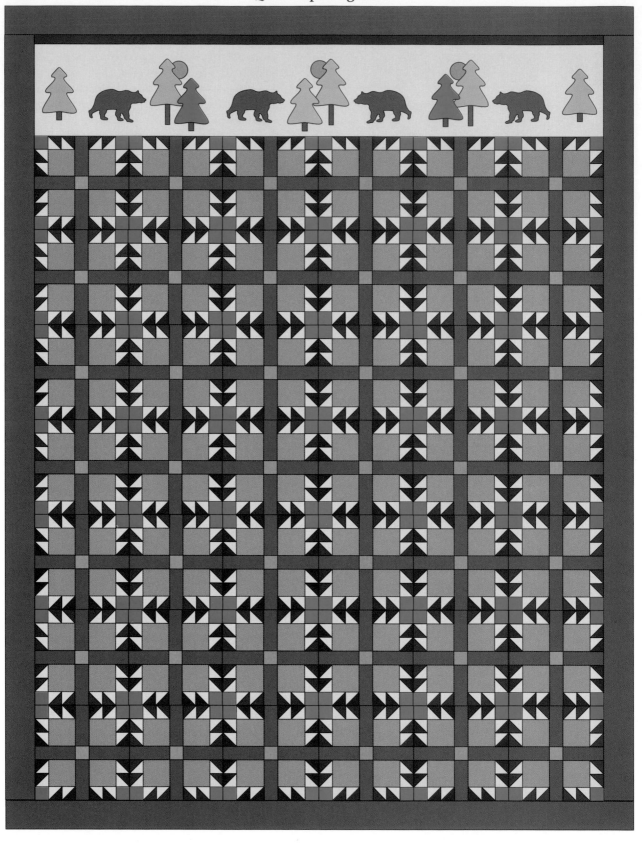

ADIRONDACK WALL HANGING

SKILL LEVEL: 1 2 **3** 4 5
BLOCK SIZE: 12¼" x 12¼"
WALL HANGING SIZE: 32" x 32"

YARDAGE REQUIREMENTS

Yardage is based on 45"w fabric.

- ⅝ yd **each** of dark brown check and light brown plaid
- ¼ yd **each** of green stripe, plaid, and solid
- 1 fat quarter (18" x 22" piece) **each** of tan print and red print
- scraps of gold plaid, green print, and dark red print
  1 yd for backing
  ½ yd for binding
  36" x 36" batting
  paper-backed fusible web
  transparent monofilament thread for appliqué

CUTTING OUT THE PIECES

All measurements include a ¼" seam allowance. Follow Rotary Cutting, page 112, to cut fabric.

1. **From dark brown check:**
   - Cut 4 strips 4" x 25" for **borders**.

2. **From light brown plaid:**
   - Cut 1 strip 4"w. From this strip, cut 8 **small squares** 4" x 4".
   - Cut 1 strip 11"w. From this strip, cut 2 **large squares** 11" x 11".

3. **From green stripe:**
   - Cut 2 strips 2¼"w. From these strips, cut 8 **rectangles** 2¼" x 5¾".

4. **From green plaid:**
   - Cut 4 squares 4" x 4" for **border squares**.

5. **From green solid:**
   - Cut 1 strip 2¼"w. From this strip, cut 10 **squares** 2¼" x 2¼".

6. **From tan print:**
   - Cut 1 **large rectangle** 12" x 20" for triangle-squares.

7. **From red print:**
   - Cut 1 **large rectangle** 12" x 20" for triangle-squares.

8. **From gold plaid:**
   - Cut 2 **squares** 2¼" x 2¼".

PREPARING THE APPLIQUÉS

Follow Preparing Appliqué Pieces, page 116, to cut pieces using patterns, pages 69 - 71.

1. **From dark brown check:**
   - Cut 1 **Bear**.

2. **From green plaid:**
   - Cut 2 **Tree A's**.

3. **From gold plaid:**
   - Cut 2 **Large Moons**.

4. **From green print:**
   - Cut 1 **Tree A**.

5. **From dark red print:**
   - Cut 1 **Small Tree Trunk**.
   - Cut 1 **Large Tree Trunk**.

ASSEMBLING THE WALL HANGING TOP

Follow Piecing and Pressing, page 114, to make wall hanging top.

1. Assemble 2 **rectangles** and 1 **square** to make **Unit 1**. Make 2 **Unit 1's**.

Unit 1 (make 2)

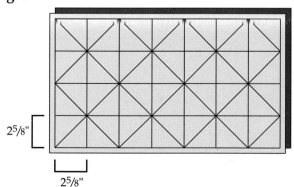

2. To make triangle-squares, place 1 tan print and 1 red print **large rectangle** right sides together. Referring to **Fig. 1**, follow Steps 1 - 3 of **Making Triangle-Squares**, page 115, to draw a grid of 28 squares 2⅝" x 2⅝". Referring to **Fig. 2,** page 66, for stitching direction, follow Steps 4 - 6 of **Making Triangle-Squares** to make a total of 56 **triangle-squares**.

Fig. 1

2⅝"

2⅝"

Fig. 2

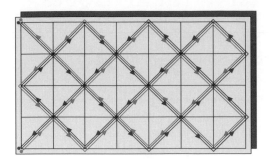

triangle-square (make 56)

3. Follow Steps 4 - 8 of **Assembling the Quilt Top** for **Adirondack Quilt**, page 62, to make 2 **Block A's**. (You will need 2 **Unit 1's**, 8 **Unit 2's**, 8 **Unit 3's**, and 4 **Unit 5's** to complete Block A's.)

4. Assemble 6 **triangle-squares** to make **Unit 6**. Make 2 **Unit 6's**. Assemble 6 **triangle-squares** and 1 **square** to make **Unit 7**. Make 2 **Unit 7's**.

Unit 6 (make 2)

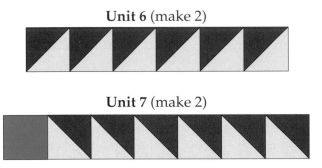

Unit 7 (make 2)

5. Assemble 1 **Unit 6**, 1 **Unit 7**, and 1 **large square** to make **Block B**. Make 2 **Block B's**.

Block B (make 2)

6. Referring to **Wall Hanging Top Diagram**, follow **Almost Invisible Appliqué**, page 116, to stitch appliqués to **Block B's**.

7. Referring to **Wall Hanging Top Diagram**, assemble **Block A's** and **Block B's** to make center section of wall hanging top.

8. Sew 2 **borders** to top and bottom of center section of wall hanging top.

9. Sew 1 **border square** to each end of remaining **borders**. Sew **borders** to sides of center section to complete **Wall Hanging Top**.

COMPLETING THE WALL HANGING

1. Follow **Quilting**, page 118, to mark, layer, and quilt, using **Quilting Diagram** as a suggestion. Our wall hanging is hand quilted.

2. Trim backing and batting even with edges of wall hanging top.

3. Follow **Making a Hanging Sleeve**, page 124, to attach hanging sleeve to wall hanging back.

4. Cut an 18" square of binding fabric. Follow **Binding**, page 122, to bind wall hanging using 2"w bias binding with mitered corners.

Wall Hanging Top Diagram

Quilting Diagram

COZY FLOOR PILLOW

BLOCK SIZE: 12¼" x 12¼"
PILLOW SIZE: 29" x 29"

YARDAGE REQUIREMENTS
Yardage is based on 45"w fabric.

- ⬛ ⅝ yd of dark brown check
- ⬜ ½ yd of tan print
- ⬛ ⅛ yd of green solid
- ⬛ 1 fat quarter (18" x 22" piece) **each** of red print and dark red print
- ⬛ 1 fat quarter (18" x 22" piece) **each** of 4 different plaids, strips, and/or checks
- ⬛ 6" x 13" piece of gold plaid
- 1 yd for pillow top backing
- 1 yd for pillow back
- 3½ yds of 2⅜"w bias strip for welting
- 3¾ yds of ⅜" cord for welting
- 32" x 32" batting
- 28" x 28" pillow form

CUTTING OUT THE PIECES
All measurements include a ¼" seam allowance. Follow
Rotary Cutting, page 112, to cut fabric.

1. **From dark brown check:** ⬛
   - Cut 2 strips 2¼"w. From these strips, cut 8 **rectangles** 2¼" x 5¾".
   - Cut 2 **strips** 5¾" x 12".
   - Cut 2 strips 2½" x 28½" for **top/bottom borders**.
   - Cut 2 strips 2½" x 25" for **side borders**.

2. **From tan print:** ⬜
   - Cut 2 **squares** 12" x 12" for triangle-squares.

3. **From green solid:** ⬛
   - Cut 1 strip 2¼"w. From this strip, cut 16 **squares** 2¼" x 2¼".

4. **From red print:** ⬛
   - Cut 1 **square** 12" x 12" for triangle-squares.

5. **From dark red print:** ⬛
   - Cut 1 **square** 12" x 12" for triangle-squares.

6. **From *each* plaid, stripe, and/or check:** ⬛
   - Cut 4 **squares** 4" x 4".

7. **From gold plaid:** ⬛
   - Cut 1 **strip** 2¼" x 12".

ASSEMBLING THE PILLOW TOP
Follow Piecing and Pressing, page 114, to make pillow top.

1. Using 12"l **strips**, follow Step 1 of **Assembling the Quilt Top** for **Adirondack Quilt**, page 61, to make 4 **Unit 1's**.

2. To make triangle-square A's, place 1 tan print and 1 red print **square** right sides together. Referring to **Fig. 1**, follow Steps 1 - 3 of **Making Triangle-Squares**, page 115, to draw a grid of 16 squares 2⅝" x 2⅝". Referring to **Fig. 2** for stitching direction, follow Steps 4 - 6 of **Making Triangle-Squares** to complete 32 **triangle-square A's**.

Fig. 1

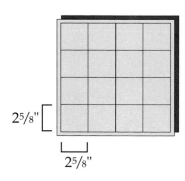

Fig. 2

triangle-square A (make 32)

3. Using remaining tan print and dark red print **squares**, repeat Step 2 to make 32 **triangle-square B's**.

triangle-square B (make 32)

4. Follow Steps 4 - 8 of **Assembling the Quilt Top** for **Adirondack Quilt**, page 62, to make 2 **Block A's**. (You will need 2 **Unit 1's**, 8 **Unit 2's**, 8 **Unit 3's**, and 4 **Unit 5's** to complete Block A's.)

5. Use **triangle-square B's** and follow Steps 4 - 8 of **Assembling the Quilt Top** for **Adirondack Quilt**, page 62, to make 2 **Block B's**. (You will need 2 **Unit 1's**, 8 **Unit 2's**, 8 **Unit 3's**, and 4 **Unit 5's** to complete Block B's.)

6. Referring to **Pillow Top Diagram**, assemble **Block A's** and **Block B's** to complete center section of pillow top.
7. Attach **side**, then **top** and **bottom borders** to complete **Pillow Top**.

COMPLETING THE PILLOW
1. Follow **Quilting**, page 118, to mark, layer, and quilt, using **Quilting Diagram**, page 63, as a suggestion. Our pillow top is hand quilted.
2. Follow **Pillow Finishing**, page 124, to complete pillow with welting.

Pillow Top Diagram

GRIZZLY BEAR SWEATER

SUPPLIES
1 sweater
10" x 10" square **each** of dark red print, light brown plaid, and green print
1½ yds of 1½"w bias strip for binding
paper-backed fusible web
embroidery floss

MAKING THE SWEATER
1. Cut 1 square 8⅞" x 8⅞" from dark red print. Cut square once diagonally to make 2 triangles. Repeat to cut 2 green print triangles.
2. Follow **Piecing and Pressing**, page 114, to assemble 1 dark red print and 1 green print triangle to make 1 **square**. (Remaining triangles will not be used.)
3. For binding, press bias strip in half lengthwise with wrong sides together and follow Steps 1 - 7 of **Attaching Binding with Mitered Corners**, page 123, to attach binding to square. Press binding out. Do not fold over to back of square.
4. Use **Bear** pattern, page 70, and follow **Preparing Appliqué Pieces**, page 116, to cut 1 bear from light brown plaid.
5. Referring to photo, fuse bear to square. Use 2 strands of floss to work **Blanket Stitch**, page 125, around edges of bear.

6. Baste square to sweater front.
7. Use 3 strands of floss to work **Blanket Stitch**, page 125, around edges of square. Remove basting stitches.

EVERGREEN SWEATER

SUPPLIES
1 sweater
assorted scraps for appliqués
paper-backed fusible web
embroidery floss

MAKING THE SWEATER
1. Use **Tree A**, **Tree B**, **Tree C**, **Large Moon**, **Small Tree Trunk**, **Medium Tree Trunk**, and **Large Tree Trunk** patterns, pages 69 - 71, and follow **Preparing Appliqué Pieces**, page 116, to cut 1 appliqué from each pattern.
2. Referring to photo, fuse appliqués to sweater.
3. Use 2 strands of floss to work **Blanket Stitch**, page 125, around edges of appliqués.

WINTER CHILL STOPPERS

SUPPLIES
scarf, gloves, and/or mittens
assorted scraps for appliqués
paper-backed fusible web
embroidery floss

MAKING THE CHILL STOPPERS
1. Referring to photo, use desired patterns, pages 70 - 71, and follow **Preparing Appliqué Pieces**, page 116, to cut appliqués from scraps.
2. Referring to photo, fuse appliqués to scarf, gloves, or mittens.
3. Use 2 strands of floss to work **Blanket Stitch**, page 125, around edges of appliqués.

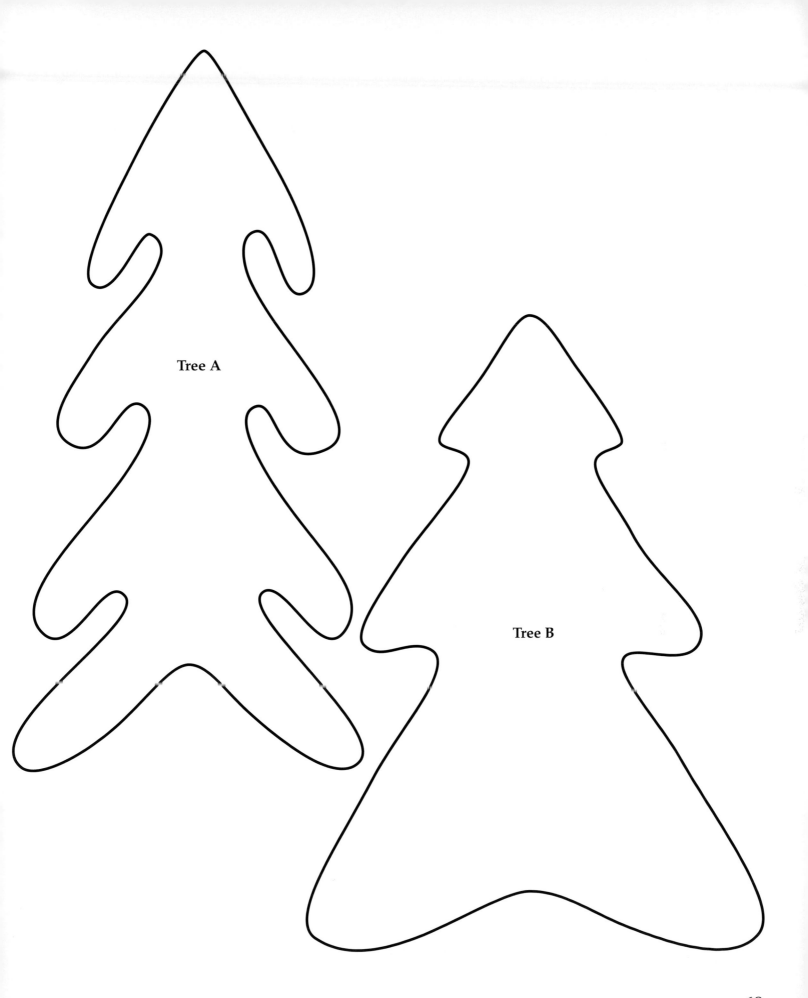

Tree A

Tree B

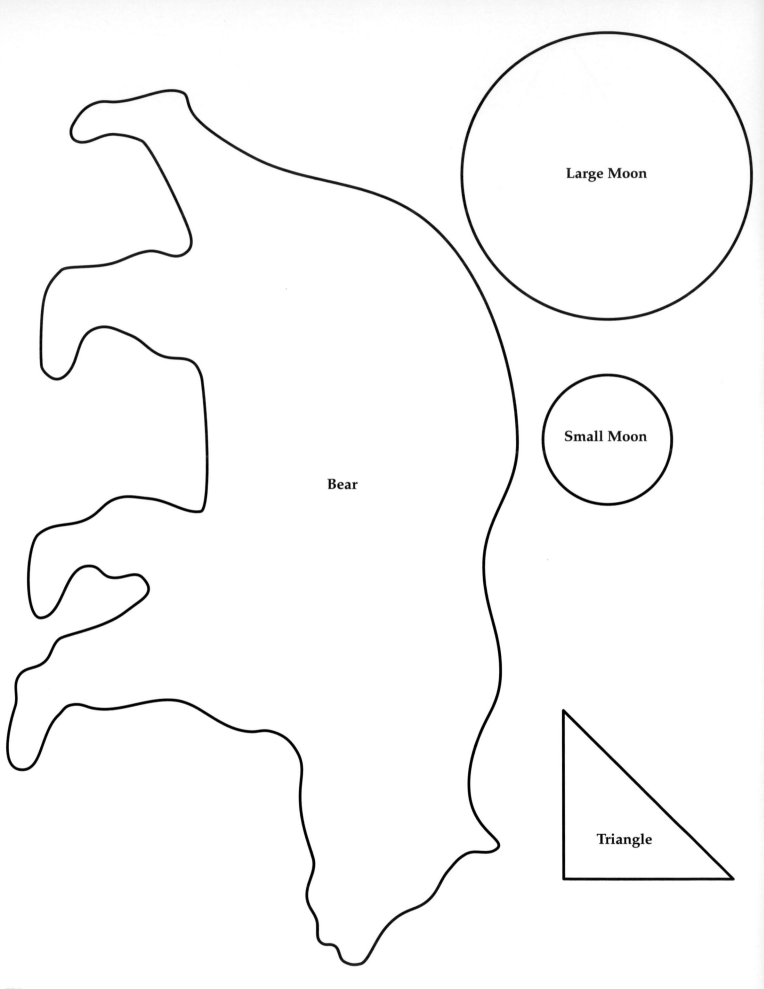

Large Moon

Small Moon

Bear

Triangle

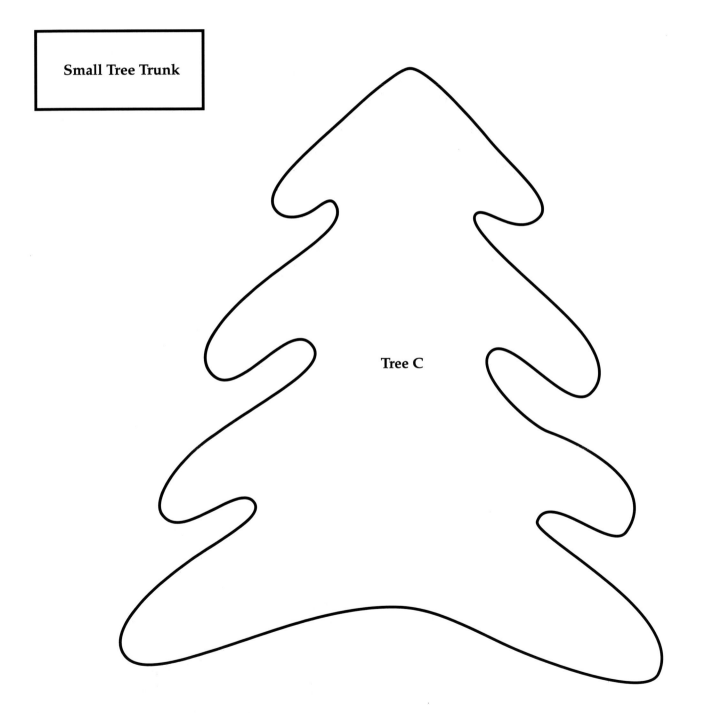

Large Tree Trunk

Medium Tree Trunk

Small Tree Trunk

Tree C

crosses
and
losses

as *Amish congregations moved into the Midwest, the cold winters inspired pioneer quilters to use their skills and creativity to produce blankets that were both warm and beautiful. Because quilting became such an important part of daily life, church districts soon developed their own unique customs, especially those regarding quilt patterns and colors. This Crosses and Losses quilt is typical of the designs made by Amish quilters in Ohio during the late 1800's. The seamstresses often used black as a main background color and alternated pieced blocks with plain squares. Our version of the simple pattern is made with an easy grid method for the triangle-squares. Complemented by a red inner border, the quilt has ample areas for beautiful feather wreath and cable quilting.*

CROSSES AND LOSSES QUILT

SKILL LEVEL: 1 2 3 4 5
BLOCK SIZE: 9" x 9"
QUILT SIZE: 95" x 108"

Because of the quick methods used to duplicate the scrappy look of our quilt, you will have some pieces left over after assembling the blocks.

YARDAGE REQUIREMENTS
Yardage is based on 45"w fabric.

☐ 7³⁄₄ yds of cream solid

■ 2⁷⁄₈ yds of dark red print

◩ 1 fat quarter (18" x 22" piece) *each* of
    11 assorted prints
    8³⁄₈ yds for backing
    1¹⁄₈ yds for binding
    120" x 120" batting

CUTTING OUT THE PIECES
All measurements include a ¼" seam allowance. Follow **Rotary Cutting**, *page 112, to cut fabric.*

1. **From cream solid:** ☐
   - Cut 4 strips 11"w. From these strips, cut 11 **rectangles** 11" x 14" for triangle-squares.
   - Cut 12 strips 2³⁄₄"w. From these strips, cut 168 **squares** 2³⁄₄" x 2³⁄₄".
   - Cut 7 strips 3¹⁄₈"w. From these strips, cut 84 squares 3¹⁄₈" x 3¹⁄₈". Cut squares once diagonally to make 168 **small triangles**.
   - Cut 8 strips 9¹⁄₂"w. From these strips, cut 30 **setting squares** 9¹⁄₂" x 9¹⁄₂".
   - Cut 4 lengthwise **outer borders** 7" x 98".
   - From remaining fabric width, cut 6 squares 14" x 14". Cut squares twice diagonally to make 24 **side triangles**. (You will need 22 and have 2 left over.)
   - From remaining fabric width, cut 2 squares 7¹⁄₄" x 7¹⁄₄". Cut squares once diagonally to make 4 **corner triangles**.

2. **From dark red print:** ■
   - Cut 2 lengthwise **inner side borders** 2³⁄₄" x 94".
   - Cut 2 lengthwise **inner top/bottom borders** 2³⁄₄" x 85".

3. **From *each* of 11 assorted prints:** ◩
   - Cut 1 **rectangle** 11" x 14" for triangle-squares.
   - Cut 4 squares 5³⁄₈" x 5³⁄₈". Cut squares once diagonally to make 8 **large triangles**.

ASSEMBLING THE QUILT TOP
Follow **Piecing and Pressing**, *page 114, to make quilt top.*

1. To make triangle-squares, place 1 print and 1 cream **rectangle** right sides together. Referring to **Fig. 1**, follow **Making Triangle-Squares**, page 115, to make 24 **triangle-squares**.

Fig. 1

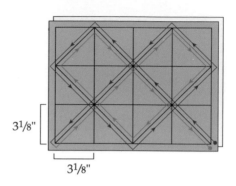

3¹⁄₈"
3¹⁄₈"

triangle-square (make 24)

2. Sew 2 **triangle-squares** and 2 **squares** together to make **Unit 1**. Make 8 **Unit 1's**.

Unit 1 (make 8)

3. Sew 1 **triangle-square** and 2 **small triangles** together to make **Unit 2**. Make 8 **Unit 2's**.

Unit 2 (make 8)

4. Sew 1 **large triangle** and 1 **Unit 2** together to make **Unit 3**. Make 8 **Unit 3's**.

Unit 3 (make 8)

5. Sew 2 **Unit 3's** and 2 **Unit 1's** together to make **Block**. Make 4 **Blocks**.

Block (make 4)

6. Repeat Steps 1 - 5 to make a total of 42 **Blocks**.
7. Referring to **Assembly Diagram**, sew **corner triangles**, **side triangles**, **Blocks**, and **setting squares** together into diagonal rows. Sew rows together to make center section of quilt top.
8. Follow **Adding Squared Borders**, page 117, to sew **side**, then **top** and **bottom inner borders** to center section. Repeat to add **outer borders** to complete **Quilt Top**.

COMPLETING THE QUILT

1. Follow **Quilting**, page 118, to mark, layer, and quilt using **Quilting Diagram** as a suggestion. Our quilt is hand quilted.
2. Cut a 34" square of binding fabric. Follow **Binding**, page 122, to bind quilt using 2¹/₂"w bias binding with mitered corners.

Quilting Diagram

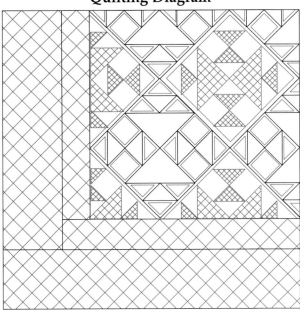

Assembly Diagram

Quilt Top Diagram

75

log cabin

a *nice fireside companion, the Log Cabin quilt dates back to Civil War days when Americans became fascinated with President Abraham Lincoln's humble beginnings in a cabin. Traditional Log Cabin blocks begin with a center square of red fabric to represent the fireplace that was always the heart of the home. To make our Sunshine and Shadows variation even easier, we sewed the "logs" around the center square and then rotary cut them to an exact fit — so there are no tiny pieces to handle! Our nifty grid method makes the Sawtooth border a breeze to piece, too.*

LOG CABIN QUILT

SKILL LEVEL: 1 2 3 4 5
BLOCK SIZE: 10" x 10"
QUILT SIZE: 91" x 111"

YARDAGE REQUIREMENTS

Yardage is based on 45"w fabric.

- ¼ yd of red
- 3¼ yds **total** of assorted dark prints
- 3 yds **total** of assorted light prints
- 3⅝ yds of tan print for narrow borders
- 1⅛ yds of dark red for pieced border
- 1⅛ yds of grey for pieced border
- 3⅝ yds of floral print for outer border
  8¼ yds for backing
  1 yd for binding
  120" x 120" batting

CUTTING OUT THE PIECES

All measurements include a ¼" seam allowance. Follow
***Rotary Cutting**, page 112, to cut fabric.*

1. **From red:**
   - Cut 3 strips 2½"w. From these strips, cut a total of 48 squares 2½" x 2½" for **center squares**.

2. **From assorted dark prints:**
   - Cut a total of 70 **strips** 1½"w.

3. **From assorted light prints:**
   - Cut a total of 60 **strips** 1½"w.

4. **From tan print:**
   - Cut 2 lengthwise strips 3" x 69" for **first (inner) top/bottom borders**.
   - Cut 2 lengthwise strips 3" x 89" for **first side borders**.
   - Cut 2 lengthwise strips 3" x 94" for **third top/bottom borders**.
   - Cut 2 lengthwise strips 3" x 114" for **third side borders**.

5. **From dark red:**
   - Cut 2 **rectangles** 19" x 31" for triangle-squares.

6. **From grey:**
   - Cut 2 **rectangles** 19" x 31" for triangle-squares.
   - Cut 4 squares 5½" x 5½" for **border corner squares**.

7. **From floral print:**
   - Cut 2 lengthwise strips 5½" x 94" for **fourth top/bottom borders**.
   - Cut 2 lengthwise strips 5½" x 114" for **fourth side borders**.

ASSEMBLING THE QUILT TOP

*Follow **Piecing and Pressing**, page 114, to make quilt top.*

1. Place 1 light print **strip** on 1 **center square** with right sides together and matching 1 long raw edge of strip with 1 raw edge of square. Stitch as shown in **Fig. 1**. Trim strip even with square (**Fig. 2**); open and press (**Fig. 3**).

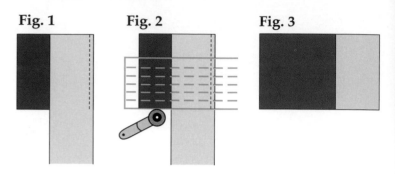

Fig. 1   **Fig. 2**   **Fig. 3**

2. Turning center square ¼ turn to the left, use a different light print **strip** and repeat Step 1 to add the next "log" as shown in **Figs. 4 - 6**.

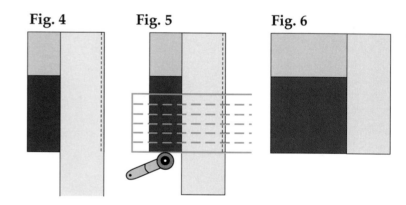

Fig. 4   **Fig. 5**   **Fig. 6**

3. Repeat Step 2, adding 2 different dark print **strips** to remaining 2 sides of center square (**Fig. 7**).

Fig. 7

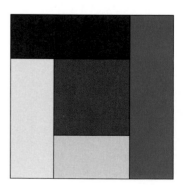

4. Continue to add **strips**, alternating 2 light and 2 dark strips until there are 4 strips on each side of center square to complete **Block**.

Block (make 48)

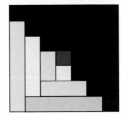

5. Repeat Steps 1 - 4 to make 48 **Blocks**.
6. Assemble 6 **Blocks** as shown to make **Row**. Make 8 **Rows**.

Row (make 8)

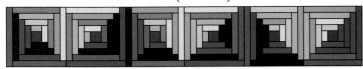

7. Referring to **Quilt Top Diagram**, page 82, assemble **Rows** to complete center section of quilt top.
8. Follow **Adding Mitered Borders**, page 118, to add **first border**.
9. To make triangle-squares, place 1 dark red and 1 grey **rectangle** right sides together. Referring to **Fig. 8**, follow Steps 1 - 3 of **Making Triangle-Squares**, page 115, to mark a grid of 15 squares 5⅞" x 5⅞". Referring to **Fig. 9** for sewing directions, follow Steps 4 - 6 of **Making Triangle-Squares**, page 115, to complete 30 triangle-squares. Repeat with remaining **rectangles** to make a total of 60 **triangle-squares**.

Fig. 8

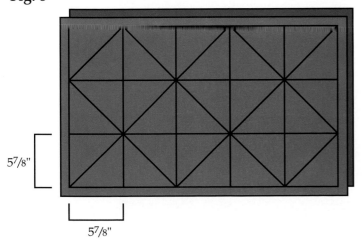

5⅞"

5⅞"

Fig. 9

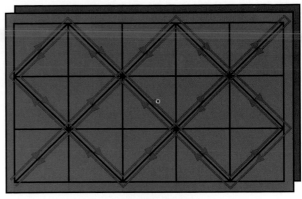

triangle-square (make 60)

10. Assemble 17 **triangle-squares** as shown to make **Second Side Border**. Make 2 **Second Side Borders**.

Second Side Border (make 2)

11. Assemble 2 **border corner squares** and 13 **triangle-squares** as shown to make **Second Top/Bottom Border**. Make 2 **Second Top/Bottom Borders**.

Second Top/Bottom Border (make 2)

12. Sew **Second Side Borders**, then **Second Top/Bottom Borders** to center section of quilt top.
13. Assemble **third** and **fourth borders** as shown to make **Border Unit**. Make 2 **Top/Bottom Border Units** and 2 **Side Border Units**.

Border Unit

14. Follow **Adding Mitered Borders**, page 118, to attach **Border Units** to center section of quilt top to complete **Quilt Top**.

COMPLETING THE QUILT

1. Follow **Quilting**, page 118, and **Quilting Diagram** and use **Wave Quilting Pattern**, page 86, and **Small** and **Large Cable Quilting Patterns**, page 87, to mark, layer, and quilt. Our quilt is hand quilted.
2. Cut a 36" square of binding fabric. Follow **Making Continuous Bias Strip Binding**, page 122, to make approximately 12 yds of 2½"w bias binding.
3. Follow **Attaching Binding with Mitered Corners**, page 123, to attach binding to quilt.

Quilting Diagram

Quilt Top Diagram

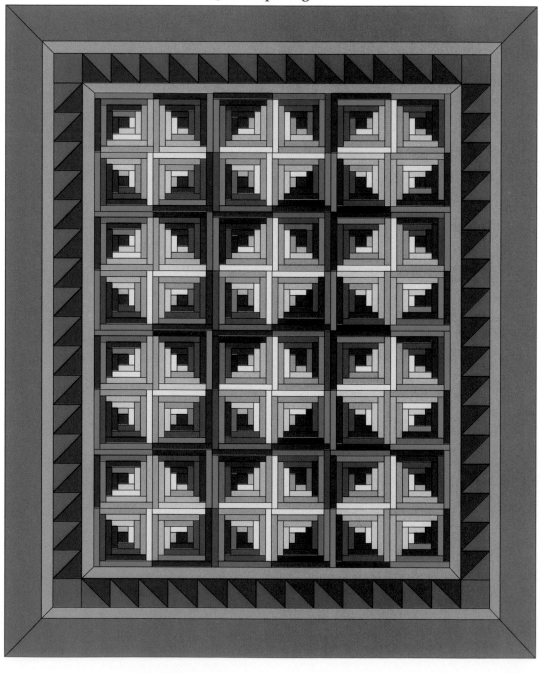

LOG CABIN WALL HANGING

SKILL LEVEL: 1 2 3 4 5
BLOCK SIZE: 7" x 7"
WALL HANGING SIZE: 43" x 43"

YARDAGE REQUIREMENTS

Yardage is based on 45"w fabric.

- ◼ 1/8 yd of red
- ◼ 1 1/4 yds **total** of assorted dark prints
- ◻ 7/8 yd **total** of assorted cream prints
- ◪ 3/4 yd **total** of assorted tan prints
- ◪ scraps for appliqués
  3 yds for backing and hanging sleeve
  3/4 yd for binding
  45" x 60" batting

You will also need:
  paper-backed fusible web
  transparent monofilament thread for appliqué

CUTTING OUT THE PIECES

All measurements include a 1/4" seam allowance. Follow Rotary Cutting, page 112, to cut fabric.

1. **From red:** ◼
   - Cut 2 strips 1 1/2"w. From these strips, cut 32 squares 1 1/2" x 1 1/2" for **center squares**.

2. **From assorted dark prints:** ◼
   - Cut a total of 27 **strips** 1 1/2"w.

3. **From assorted cream prints:** ◻
   - Cut 1 square 14 1/2" x 14 1/2" from 1 print for **center block**.
   - Cut a total of 9 **strips** 1 1/2"w.

4. **From assorted tan prints:** ◪
   - Cut a total of 14 **strips** 1 1/2"w.

5. **From scraps:** ◪
   - Cut 1 bias strip 1/2" x 13" and 4 bias strips 1/2" x 7" for **vines**.
   - Referring to photo, follow **Preparing Appliqué Pieces**, page 116, to cut the following number of pieces from **Appliqué Patterns**, pages 86 and 87:
     - Flowers — 14
     - Flower Centers — 14
     - Leaves — 28
     - Vine Heart — 16
     - Roof — 1
     - Gable — 1
     - House Heart — 1
     - House Front — 1 rectangle 4" x 6"

House Side — 1 rectangle 5" x 6"
Door — 1 rectangle 1 1/2" x 4"
Chimney — 1 rectangle 1" x 1 3/4"
Windows — 2 rectangles 1 1/2" x 2"

ASSEMBLING THE WALL HANGING TOP

Follow Piecing and Pressing, page 114, to make wall hanging top.

1. Refer to **Wall Hanging Top Diagram**, page 84, and follow **Almost Invisible Appliqué**, page 116, to appliqué house pieces only to **center block**.

2. Follow Steps 1 - 4 of **Assembling the Quilt Top** for **Log Cabin Quilt**, page 80, to make 12 **Block A's** as shown using cream and dark strips and 20 **Block B's** as shown using tan and dark strips. (*Note:* The blocks for the **Log Cabin Wall Hanging** use smaller center squares than those in the **Log Cabin Quilt** and have 3 strips on each side of the center square instead of 4.)

Block A (make 12)   Block B (make 20)

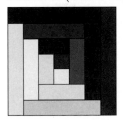   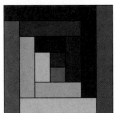

3. Assemble 6 **Block B's** as shown to make **Unit 1**. Make 2 **Unit 1's**.

Unit 1 (make 2)

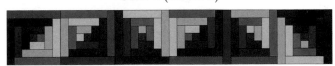

4. Assemble 2 **Block B's** and 4 **Block A's** as shown to make **Unit 2**. Make 2 **Unit 2's**.

Unit 2 (make 2)

5. Assemble 2 **Block B's** and 2 **Block A's** as shown to make **Unit 3**. Make 2 **Unit 3's**.

Unit 3 (make 2)

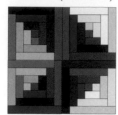

6. Referring to **Wall Hanging Top Diagram**, assemble **Unit 1's**, **Unit 2's**, **Unit 3's**, and **center block**.
7. Referring to **Wall Hanging Top Diagram**, hand baste **vines** in place; fuse remaining appliqué pieces in place. Follow **Almost Invisible Appliqué**, page 116, to appliqué **vines**, **flowers**, **leaves**, and **vine hearts** to complete **Wall Hanging Top**.

COMPLETING THE WALL HANGING

1. Follow **Quilting**, page 118, and **Quilting Diagram** to mark, layer, and quilt. Our wall hanging is hand quilted.
2. Follow **Making a Hanging Sleeve**, page 124, to attach hanging sleeve to wall hanging back.
3. Cut a 27" square of binding fabric. Follow **Making Continuous Bias Strip Binding**, page 122, to make approximately 5 1/4 yds of 2 1/2"w bias binding.
4. Follow **Attaching Binding with Mitered Corners**, page 123, to attach binding to wall hanging.

Quilting Diagram

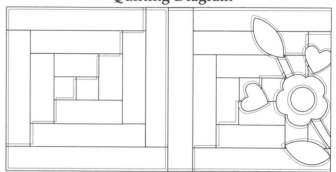

Wall Hanging Top Diagram

LOG CABIN PILLOW

PILLOW SIZE: 18" x 18"

YARDAGE REQUIREMENTS

Yardage is based on 45"w fabric.

- 12½" x 12½" square of cream print fabric
- scraps for appliqués and borders
  21½" x 21½" square for pillow top backing
  19" x 19" square for pillow back
  3" x 76" bias strip (pieced if necessary) for welting

You will also need:
    paper-backed fusible web
    21½" x 21½" batting
    2⅛ yds of ½" cord for welting
    transparent monofilament thread for appliqué
    polyester fiberfill

MAKING THE PILLOW

1. Follow **Preparing Appliqué Pieces**, page 116, to cut out house shapes listed in Step 5 of **Cutting Out the Pieces** for **Log Cabin Wall Hanging**, page 83.
2. Refer to **Pillow Top Diagram** and follow **Almost Invisible Appliqué**, page 116, to appliqué house pieces to 12½" x 12½" square.
3. For inner borders, cut scraps into 2"w strips that vary in length from 3" to 8". Referring to **Pillow Top Diagram**, assemble strips, trim to fit, and sew to sides, then top and bottom of 12½" x 12½" square. Repeat for outer borders.
4. Follow **Quilting**, page 118, to layer and quilt in the ditch around house and border pieces.
5. Follow **Pillow Finishing**, page 124, to complete pillow with welting.

Pillow Top Diagram

LOG CABIN SHUTTERS

SHUTTER SIZE: 13" x 73" each

Our shutters fit a 72"l window. For smaller or larger windows, adjust size accordingly.

YARDAGE REQUIREMENTS

Yardage is based on 45"w fabric.

- ⅛ yd of red
- 1 yd **total** of assorted dark prints
- 1 yd **total** of assorted light prints
- ½ yd of light print for borders
  2¼ yds for backing and hanging sleeves
  1 yd for binding
  72" x 90" batting

CUTTING OUT THE PIECES

All measurements include a ¼" seam allowance. Follow Rotary Cutting, page 112, to cut fabric.

1. **From red:** ▪
   - Cut 1 strip 2½"w. From this strip, cut 14 squares 2½" x 2½" for **center squares**.
2. **From assorted dark prints:** ▪
   - Cut a total of 22 **strips** 1½"w.
3. **From assorted light prints:** ▪
   - Cut a total of 18 **strips** 1½"w.
4. **From light print for borders:** ▪
   - Cut a total of 10 strips 1½"w for **borders**.

ASSEMBLING THE SHUTTER TOPS

Follow Piecing and Pressing, page 114, to make shutter tops.

1. Follow Steps 1 - 4 of **Assembling the Quilt Top** for **Log Cabin Quilt**, page 80, to make 14 **Blocks**.
2. Referring to photo, assemble 7 **Blocks** to make center section of shutter top. Make 2 center sections.
3. Piecing strips as necessary, follow **Adding Squared Borders**, page 117, to add **borders** to complete each shutter top.

COMPLETING THE SHUTTERS

1. Follow **Quilting**, page 118, and **Quilting Diagram** to mark, layer, and quilt each shutter.
2. Follow **Making a Hanging Sleeve**, page 124, to attach a hanging sleeve to each shutter.
3. Cut a 36" square of binding fabric. Follow **Making Continuous Bias Strip Binding**, page 122, to make approximately 10½ yds of 2½"w bias binding.
4. Follow **Attaching Binding with Mitered Corners**, page 123, to attach binding to each shutter.

Quilting Diagram

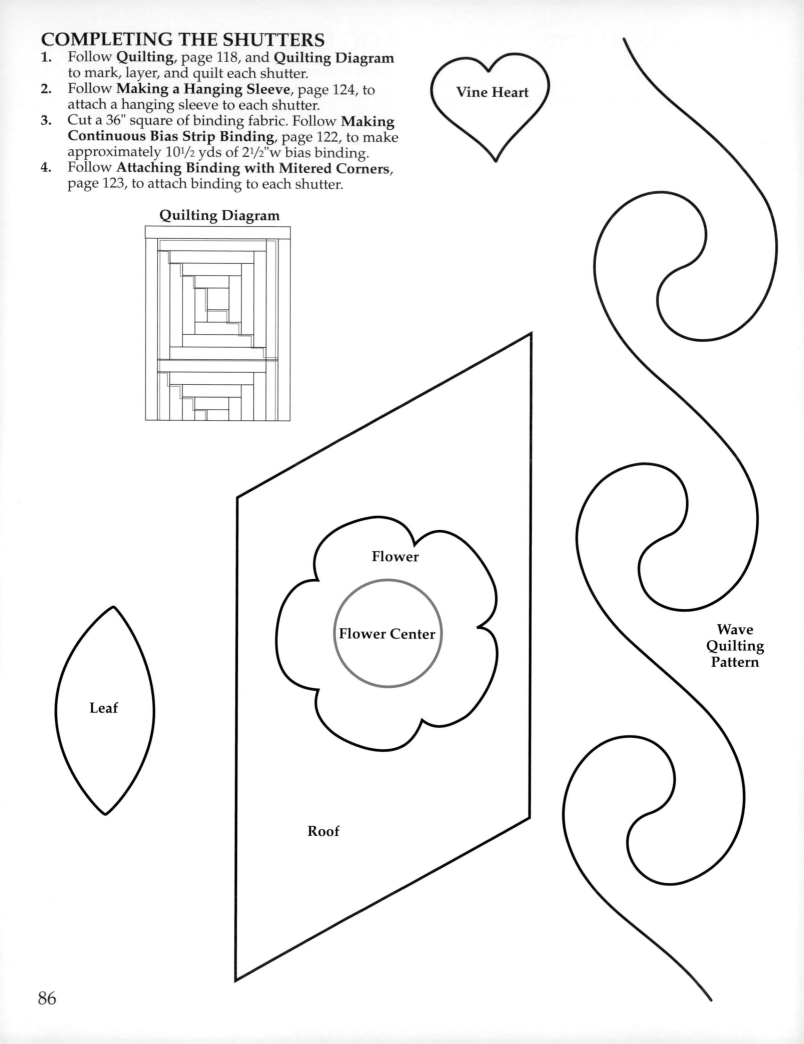

Vine Heart

Flower

Flower Center

Leaf

Roof

Wave Quilting Pattern

Gable

House Heart

Large Cable Quilting Pattern

Small Cable Quilting Pattern

87

churn dash maze

this quilt conveys the beauty and simplicity of homemade goodness, while providing the warmth of handmade love. Back in the days when families handcrafted most of their everyday supplies, mothers would spend their evenings quilting, while the youngsters often took turns pumping a churn dash to make rich cream and butter. Named for that rough-hewn tool, the Churn Dash design is a true quilting classic. The blocks in our version were made by strip-piecing the center sections and grid-piecing the triangle-square corners. The blocks were arranged with a sashing design known as Garden Maze that creates a neat frame for each square.

CHURN DASH MAZE QUILT

SKILL LEVEL: 1 2 3 4 5
BLOCK SIZE: 11¼" x 11¼"
QUILT SIZE: 74" x 90"

YARDAGE REQUIREMENTS

Yardage is based on 45"w fabric.

☐ 4¾ yds of cream solid
■ 4½ yds of dark red print
5½ yds for backing
1 yd for binding
81" x 96" batting

CUTTING OUT THE PIECES

All measurements include a ¼" seam allowance. Follow **Rotary Cutting**, *page 112, and* **Template Cutting**, *page 114, to cut fabric.*

1. **From cream solid:** ☐
   • Cut 5 **rectangles** 13" x 23" for triangle-squares.
   • Cut 9 **strips** 2¾"w.
   • Cut 17 **wide strips** 4"w.
   • Cut 4 strips 4¾"w. From these strips, cut 30 squares 4¾" x 4¾". Cut squares twice diagonally to make 120 **triangles**.

2. **From dark red print:** ■
   • Cut 5 **rectangles** 13" x 23" for triangle-squares.
   • Cut 7 **strips** 2¾"w.
   • Cut 34 **narrow strips** 1½"w.
   • Cut 60 **A's** using **Template A** pattern, page 93.
   • Cut 30 **B's** using **Template B** pattern, page 93.

ASSEMBLING THE QUILT TOP

Follow **Piecing and Pressing**, *page 114, to make quilt top.*

1. To make triangle-squares, place 1 dark red and 1 cream **rectangle** right sides together. Referring to **Fig. 1**, follow **Making Triangle-Squares**, page 115, to make 16 **triangle-squares**. Repeat with remaining **rectangles** to make a total of 80 **triangle-squares**.

Fig. 1

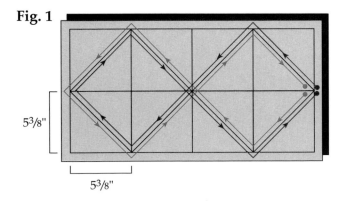

triangle-square (make 80)

2. Sew 2 **strips** together to make **Strip Set A**. Make 3 **Strip Set A's**. Cut across **Strip Set A's** at 2¾" intervals to make 40 **Unit 1's**.

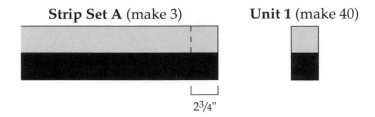

Strip Set A (make 3)   **Unit 1** (make 40)

2¾"

3. Sew 5 **strips** together to make **Strip Set B**. Make 2 **Strip Set B's**. Cut across **Strip Set B's** at 2¾" intervals to make 20 **Unit 2's**.

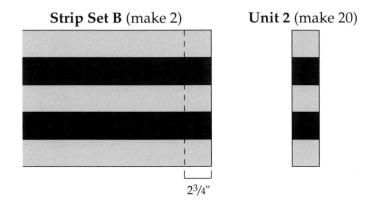

Strip Set B (make 2)   **Unit 2** (make 20)

2¾"

4. Sew 2 **triangle-squares** and 1 **Unit 1** together to make **Unit 3**. Make 40 **Unit 3's**.

Unit 3 (make 40)

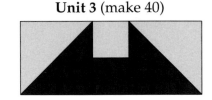

5. Sew 2 **Unit 3's** and 1 **Unit 2** together to make **Block**. Make 20 **Blocks**.

Block (make 20)

6. Sew 1 **wide** and 2 **narrow strips** together to make **Strip Set C**. Make 17 **Strip Set C's**. Cut across **Strip Set C's** at 11¾" intervals to make 49 **Sashing Units**.

Strip Set C (make 17)   **Sashing Unit** (make 49)

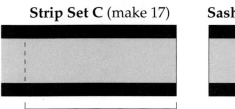

11¾"

7. Sew 2 **triangles** and 1 **A** together to make **Unit 4**. Make 60 **Unit 4's**.

Unit 4 (make 60)

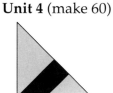

8. Sew 2 **Unit 4's** and 1 **B** together to make **Sashing Squares**. Make 30 **Sashing Squares**.

Sashing Square (make 30)

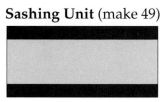

9. Sew 5 **Sashing Squares** and 4 **Sashing Units** together to make **Sashing Row**. Make 6 **Sashing Rows**.

Sashing Row (make 6)

10. Sew 5 **Sashing Units** and 4 **Blocks** together to make **Row**. Make 5 **Rows**.

Row (make 5)

11. Referring to **Quilt Top Diagram**, page 92, sew **Sashing Rows** and **Rows** together to complete **Quilt Top**.

COMPLETING THE QUILT

1. Follow **Quilting**, page 118, to mark, layer, and quilt, using **Quilting Diagram** as a suggestion. Our quilt is hand quilted.
2. Cut a 31" square of binding fabric. Follow **Binding**, page 122, to bind quilt using 2½"w bias binding with mitered corners.

Quilting Diagram

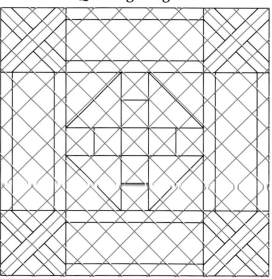

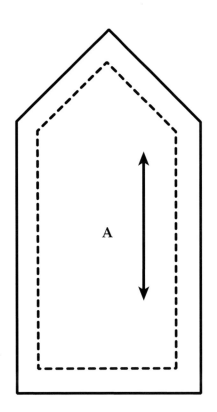

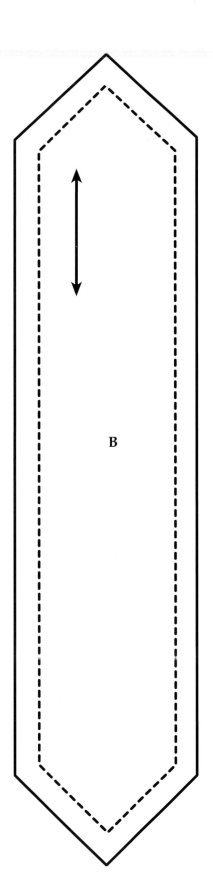

lady of the lake

ideal for snuggling together during cold-weather outings, this Lady of the Lake quilt was inspired by the romantic writings of Sir Walter Scott in the early nineteenth century. Our version of the traditional pattern was made using a variety of homey fabrics to create a quaint scrap quilt look. The eclectic arrangement of small "waves" is quite easy to construct — a quick grid technique allows you to make nearly a hundred triangle-squares at a time! For a tranquil touch, the quilt is edged with two simple borders.

LADY OF THE LAKE QUILT

SKILL LEVEL: 1 2 3 4 5
BLOCK SIZE: 6⁷/₈" x 6⁷/₈"
QUILT SIZE: 83" x 102"

Because of the quick methods used to duplicate the scrappy look of the quilt, you will have some pieces left over after assembling the blocks.

YARDAGE REQUIREMENTS
Yardage is based on 45"w fabric.

- 1 yd *each* of 12 dark prints
- 1 yd *each* of 12 light prints
- 3¼ yds of green print
- 3¼ yds of gold print
  7⁵/₈ yds for backing
  1 yd for binding
  90" x 108" batting

CUTTING OUT THE PIECES
All measurements include a ¼" seam allowance. Follow Rotary Cutting, page 112, to cut fabric.

1. **From *each* dark print:**
    - Cut 2 **large rectangles** 15" x 20" for small triangle-squares.
    - Cut 1 **small rectangle** 12" x 17" for large triangle-squares.
    - From *each* of 8 fabrics, cut 1 square 5" x 5" and 1 square 2¼" x 2¼". Cut squares once diagonally to make 16 **large triangles** and 16 **small triangles**.

2. **From *each* light print:**
    - Cut 2 **large rectangles** 15" x 20" for small triangle-squares.
    - Cut 1 **small rectangle** 12" x 17" for large triangle-squares.
    - From *each* of 8 fabrics, cut 1 square 5" x 5" and 1 square 2¼" x 2¼". Cut squares once diagonally to make 16 **large triangles** and 16 **small triangles.**

3. **From green print:**
    - Cut 2 lengthwise **side inner borders** 2½" x 105".
    - Cut 2 lengthwise **top/bottom inner borders** 2½" x 86".

4. **From gold print:**
    - Cut 2 lengthwise **side outer borders** 5¼" x 105".
    - Cut 2 lengthwise **top/bottom outer borders** 5¼" x 86".

ASSEMBLING THE QUILT TOP
Follow Piecing and Pressing, page 114, to make quilt top.

1. To make small triangle-squares, place 1 light and 1 dark **large rectangle** right sides together. Referring to **Fig. 1**, follow **Making Triangle-Squares**, page 115, to make 96 **small triangle-squares**. Using same color combination, repeat to make a total of 192 **small triangle-squares**.

Fig. 1

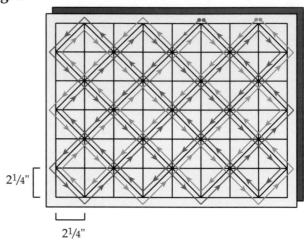

2¼"

2¼"

small triangle-square (make 192)

2. Using same color combination as in Step 1, place light and dark **small rectangles** right sides together. Referring to **Fig. 2**, follow **Making Triangle-Squares**, page 115, to make 12 **large triangle-squares**.

Fig. 2

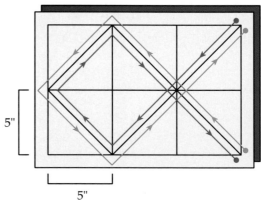

5"

5"

large triangle-square (make 12)

3. Sew 3 **small triangle-squares** together to make **Unit 1**. Make 22 **Unit 1's**. Sew 5 **small triangle-squares** together to make **Unit 2**. Make 22 **Unit 2's**.

Unit 1 (make 22)

Unit 2 (make 22)

4. Sew 2 **Unit 1's**, 1 **large triangle-square**, and 2 **Unit 2's** together to make **Block**. Make 11 **Blocks**.

Block (make 11)

5. Repeat Steps 1 - 4 to make 127 **Blocks**.
6. Sew 1 light print **small triangle** and 3 matching **small triangle-squares** together to make **Unit 3**. Sew 1 light print **small triangle** and 4 matching **small triangle-squares** together to make **Unit 4**.

Unit 3

Unit 4

7. Sew **Unit 3**, **Unit 4**, and 1 matching **large triangle** together to make **Partial Block A**.

Partial Block A

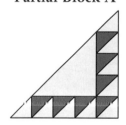

8. Repeat Steps 6 and 7 to make 8 **Partial Block A's.**
9. Using dark print **small triangles** and **large triangles**, repeat Steps 6 and 7 to make 8 **Partial Block B's**.

Partial Block B (make 8)

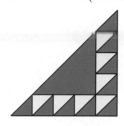

10. Referring to **Assembly Diagram**, page 98, sew **Partial Blocks** and **Blocks** into diagonal rows. Sew rows together to make center section of quilt top.
11. Referring to **Fig. 3**, place ruler on 1 side edge of quilt top with ¼" marking (shown in pink) lined up with seam intersections; trim sides of **Blocks**.

Fig. 3

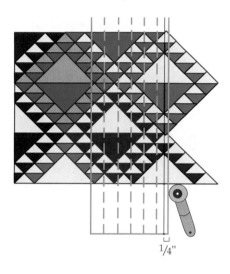

1/4"

12. Sew side **inner** and **outer borders** together along long edges to make 2 **Side Border Units**. Sew top/bottom **inner** and **outer borders** together to make 2 **Top/Bottom Border Units**.
13. Follow **Adding Mitered Borders**, page 118, to sew **Border Units** to center section to complete **Quilt Top**.

COMPLETING THE QUILT

1. Follow **Quilting**, page 118, to mark, layer, and quilt using **Quilting Diagram**, page 99, as a suggestion. Our quilt is hand quilted.
2. Cut a 32" square of binding fabric. Follow **Binding**, page 122, to bind quilt using 2½"w bias binding with mitered corners.

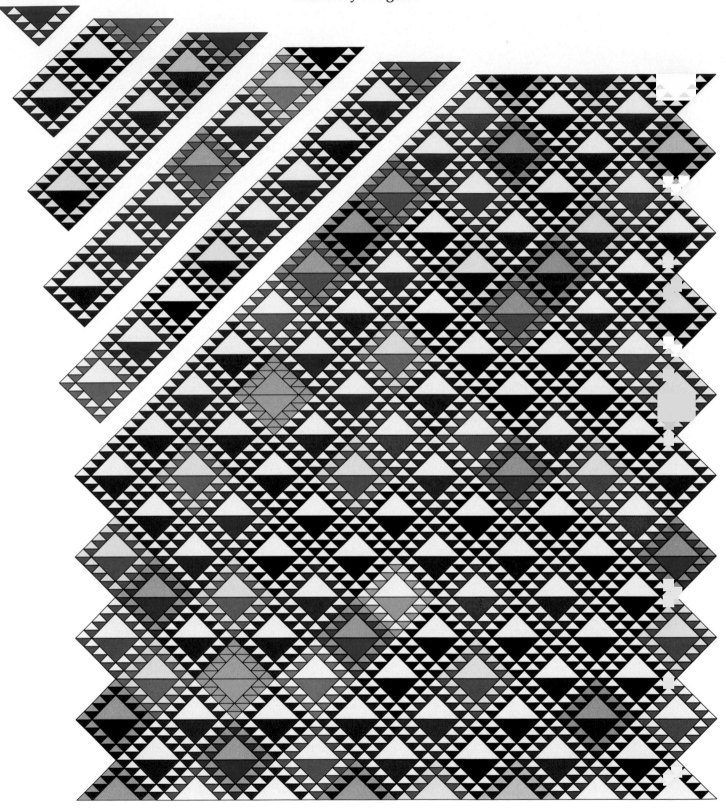

Quilt Top Diagram

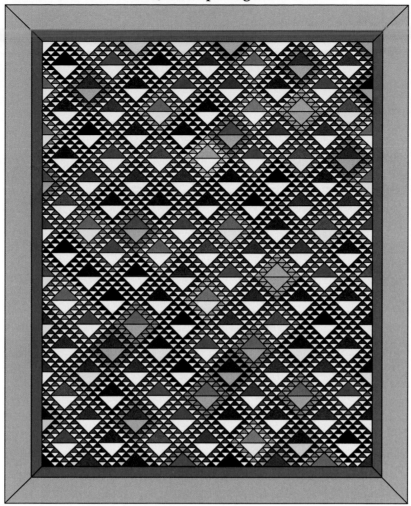

Quilting Diagram

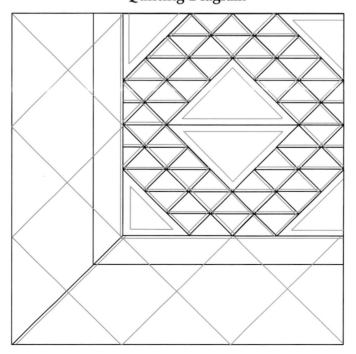

starry log cabin

*b*righten the gray days of winter with a Starry Log Cabin quilt! A hallmark of pioneer America, the log cabin became a symbol of the ingenuity and perseverance that forged the foundation for a young nation. Naturally, it also inspired one of the earliest — and most enduring — quilt patterns. Created with a medley of old-fashioned print fabrics, this cover captures the essence of life on the prairie beneath an open sky. Always loved for its simple construction, the pattern is created by stitching the "logs" around a center square and then trimming them to size. To make it even easier, we show you how to use a template with your rotary cutting ruler so you can work in the LeMoyne Stars as you go.

STARRY LOG CABIN QUILT

SKILL LEVEL: 1 2 3 4 5
BLOCK SIZE: 9" x 9"
QUILT SIZE: 88" x 106"

YARDAGE REQUIREMENTS
Yardage is based on 45"w fabric.

4¹/₂ yds total of assorted blue prints

4 yds total of assorted red prints

3³/₈ yds of floral print for borders

1 yd each of tan/red print and tan/blue print

¹/₄ yd of dark red solid
8 yds for backing
1 yd for binding
120" x 120" batting

You will also need:
tracing paper
transparent tape

CUTTING OUT THE PIECES
All measurements include a ¼" seam allowance. Follow
Rotary Cutting, *page 112, to cut fabric.*

1. **From assorted blue prints:**
   - Cut a total of 90 **strips** 1¹/₂"w.

2. **From assorted red prints:**
   - Cut a total of 80 **strips** 1¹/₂"w.

3. **From floral print for borders:**
   - Cut 2 lengthwise **side borders** 8" x 109".
   - Cut 2 lengthwise **top/bottom borders** 8" x 92".

4. **From tan/red and tan/blue print:**
   - Cut 18 **strips** 1¹/₂"w from *each* fabric.

5. **From dark red solid:**
   - Cut 3 strips 1¹/₂"w. From these strips, cut 80
     squares 1¹/₂" x 1¹/₂".

ASSEMBLING THE QUILT TOP
Follow ***Piecing and Pressing***, *page 114, to make quilt top.*

1. Referring to **Fig. 1**, align 45° marking (shown in
   pink) on ruler with lower edge of 1 tan/blue print
   strip. Cut along right edge of ruler to cut 1 end of
   strip at a 45° angle.

Fig. 1

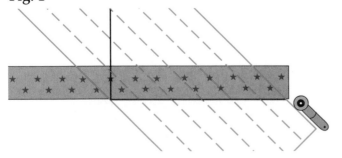

2. Turn cut **strip** 180° on mat and align 45° marking
   on ruler with lower edge of **strip**. Align the
   previously cut 45° edge with 1¹/₂" marking on ruler.
   Cut **strip** at 1¹/₂" intervals as shown in **Fig. 2** to cut
   diamonds.

Fig. 2

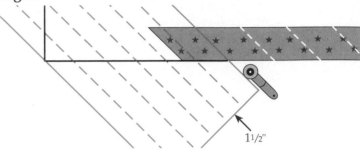

3. Using remaining tan print **strips**, repeat Steps 1
   and 2 to cut a total of 320 **diamond A's** from
   tan/blue print and 320 **diamond B's** from tan/red
   print.

diamond A (cut 320)   **diamond B** (cut 320)

4. To make paper template, carefully trace Trapezoid
   pattern, page 107, onto tracing paper; cut out on
   solid line. Use transparent tape to securely tape
   template to **wrong** side of ruler, aligning diagonal
   template edges with ruler edges (**Fig. 3**).

Fig. 3

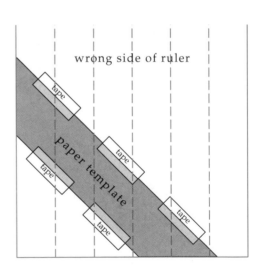

5. Place ruler template side down on 1 red print **strip**,
   aligning long edges of template with long edges of
   strip. Cut along both edges of ruler; cut 1
   trapezoid (**Fig. 4a**).

Fig. 4a

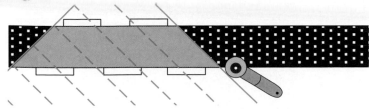

6. Turn ruler 180° and align template edges with **strip** edges to cut another **trapezoid** (**Fig. 4b**). Turning ruler after each cut, cut 6 **trapezoids** from **strip**.

Fig. 4b

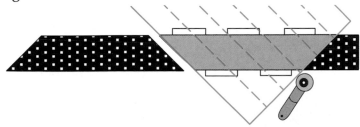

7. Using red print and blue print **strips**, repeat Steps 5 and 6 to cut a total of 160 **red trapezoids** and 160 **blue trapezoids**. (You will need 2 matching **red** and 2 matching **blue trapezoids** for each of 80 Blocks.)

red trapezoid (cut 160)

blue trapezoid (cut 160)

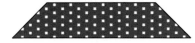

8. Sew 1 **diamond A** to left end and 1 **diamond B** to right end of 1 **red trapezoid** to make **Unit 1**. Make 160 **Unit 1's**.

Unit 1 (make 160)

9. Sew 1 **diamond A** to left end and 1 **diamond B** to right end of 1 **blue trapezoid** to make **Unit 2**. Make 160 **Unit 2's**.

Unit 2 (make 160)

10. Place 1 red print **strip** on 1 **square** with right sides together and raw edges matching. Stitch as shown in **Fig. 5a**. Trim strip even with square (**Fig. 5b**), press open (**Fig. 5c**).

Fig. 5a   **Fig. 5b**   **Fig. 5c**

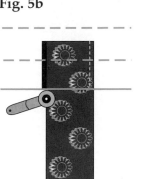      

11. Turn **square** ¼ turn to the left. Using same red print strip, repeat Step 10 to add the next "log" as shown in **Figs. 6a-6c**.

Fig. 6a   **Fig. 6b**   **Fig. 6c**

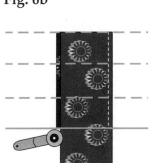      

12. Repeat Step 11, adding 2 matching blue print logs to remaining 2 sides of **square** (**Fig. 7**).

Fig. 7

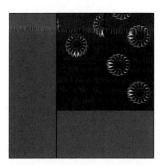

13. Continue adding **strips**, alternating 2 matching red print strips and 2 matching blue print strips until there are 3 logs on each side of square to make **Unit 3**.

Unit 3

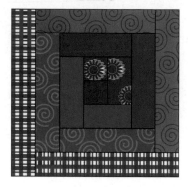

14. Repeat Steps 10 - 13 to make 80 **Unit 3's**.
15. (*Note:* Follow Steps 15 - 17 to make 80 Blocks.) Beginning and ending stitching exactly 1/4" from edges of Unit 3 and backstitching at each end, sew 1 **Unit 1** to 1 **Unit 3** (**Fig. 8**).

Fig. 8

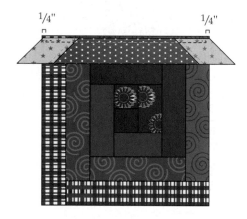

16. Repeat Step 15 to sew a matching **Unit 1**, then 2 matching **Unit 2's** to **Unit 3**, matching red trapezoids to red logs and blue trapezoids to blue logs.
17. To complete stitching at corners, fold 2 adjacent **diamonds** with right sides together and stitch from end of previous stitching to outside edge, backstitching at beginning of seam (**Fig. 9**). Repeat for remaining corners to complete **Block**.

Fig. 9

Block (make 80)

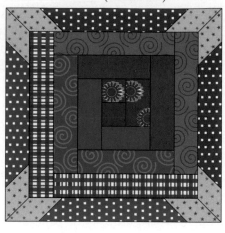

18. Sew 8 **Blocks** together to make **Row**. Make 10 **Rows**.

Row (make 10)

19. Referring to **Quilt Top Diagram**, sew **Rows** together to make center section of quilt top.
20. Follow **Adding Mitered Borders**, page 118, to sew **borders** to center section to complete **Quilt Top**.

COMPLETING THE QUILT
1. Follow **Quilting**, page 118, to mark, layer, and quilt using **Quilting Diagram** as a suggestion. Our quilt is hand quilted.
2. Cut a 32" square of binding fabric. Follow **Binding**, page 122, to bind quilt using 2¹/₂"w bias binding with mitered corners.

Quilting Diagram

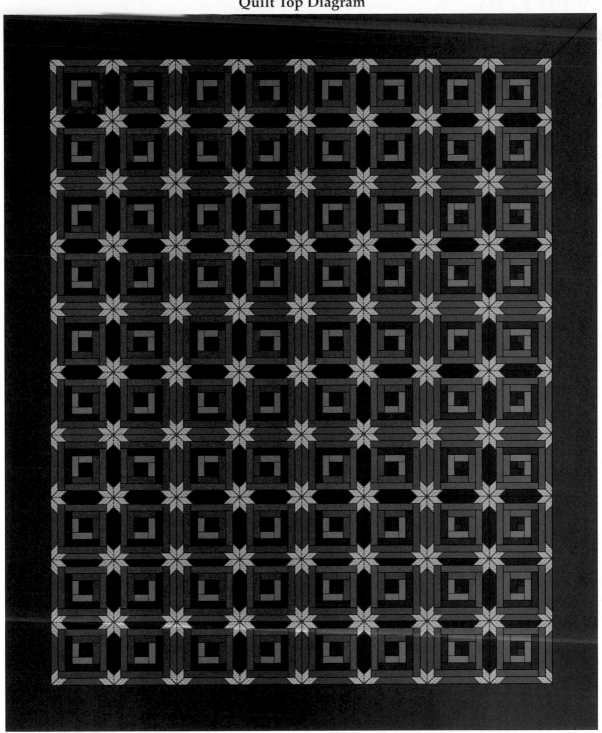

Trapezoid

THROW PILLOW

BLOCK SIZE: 9" x 9"
PILLOW SIZE: 19" x 19"

Instructions are for making 1 pillow. While our diagram shows a pillow with blue "logs" at the center, you can easily change the look of your pillow by turning the same blocks so the red logs are at the center.

SUPPLIES

- scraps of assorted red print and blue print fabrics
- scraps of tan/blue print and tan/red print fabrics
- scrap of dark red solid fabric
  22" x 22" square of fabric for backing
  5/8 yd of 45"w fabric for pillow back
  22" x 22" batting
  polyester fiberfill
  2 1/2 yds of 2"w bias fabric strip for welting
  2 1/2 yds of 1/4" cord for welting

MAKING THE PILLOW

All measurements include a 1/4" seam allowance. Follow Rotary Cutting, page 112, and Piecing and Pressing, page 114, to make pillow.

1. Cut tan/blue and tan/red print scraps into 1 1/2"w **strips**. Follow Steps 1 - 3 of **Assembling the Quilt Top**, page 104, to cut 16 **diamond A's** and 16 **diamond B's**.
2. Cut 4 assorted **strips** 1 1/2" x 15" from red print scraps. Repeat for blue print scraps. Follow Steps 4 - 7 of **Assembling the Quilt Top**, page 104, to cut 2 **trapezoids** from each **strip**. (You will need 2 matching **red** and 2 matching **blue trapezoids** for each of 4 Blocks.)
3. Follow Steps 8 and 9 of **Assembling the Quilt Top**, page 105, to make 8 **Unit 1's** and 8 **Unit 2's**.
4. Cut 4 **squares** 1 1/2" x 1 1/2" from dark red solid fabric. Cut red print and blue print scraps into 1 1/2"w **strips** for logs. (Depending on location in block, you will need strips varying in length from 5 1/2" to 16".)
5. Using **squares** and **strips**, follow Steps 10 - 13 of **Assembling the Quilt Top**, page 105, to make 4 **Unit 3's**.
6. Follow Steps 15 - 17 of **Assembling the Quilt Top**, page 106, to complete 4 **Blocks**.
7. Referring to **Pillow Top** diagram, sew **Blocks** together to make **Pillow Top**.
8. Follow **Quilting**, page 118, to mark, layer, and quilt using **Quilting Diagram**, page 106, as a suggestion. Our pillow top is hand quilted.
9. Follow **Pillow Finishing**, page 124, to complete pillow with welting.

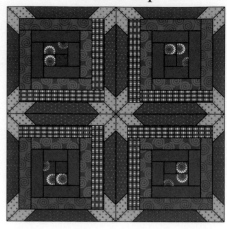

Pillow Top

STARRY WALL HANGING

SKILL LEVEL: 1 2 3 4 5
BLOCK SIZE: 9" x 9"
WALL HANGING SIZE: 25" x 52"

YARDAGE REQUIREMENTS

Yardage is based on 45"w fabric.

- 1 3/4 yds of floral print for border
- 3/4 yd total of assorted blue prints
- 5/8 yd total of assorted red prints
- 1/4 yd each of tan/red print and tan/blue print
- 1/8 yd of dark red solid
  1 5/8 yds for backing
  3/4 yd for binding
  29" x 56" batting

CUTTING OUT THE PIECES

All measurements include a 1/4" seam allowance. Follow Rotary Cutting, page 112, to cut fabric.

1. **From floral print for border:**
   - Cut 2 lengthwise **side borders** 3 3/4" x 56".
   - Cut 2 lengthwise **top/bottom borders** 3 3/4" x 29".
2. **From assorted blue prints:**
   - Cut 14 **strips** 1 1/2"w.
3. **From assorted red prints:**
   - Cut 12 **strips** 1 1/2"w.
4. **From tan/red print and tan/blue print:**
   - Cut 3 **strips** 1 1/2"w from *each* fabric.
5. **From dark red solid:**
   - Cut 10 **squares** 1 1/2" x 1 1/2".

MAKING THE WALL HANGING

*Follow **Piecing and Pressing**, page 114, to make wall hanging top.*

1. Using tan print **strips**, follow Steps 1 - 3 of **Assembling the Quilt Top**, page 104, to cut 40 **diamond A's** and 40 **diamond B's**.

2. Using red and blue print **strips**, follow Steps 4 - 7 of **Assembling the Quilt Top**, page 104, to cut 20 **red trapezoids** and 20 **blue trapezoids**. (You will need 2 matching **red** and 2 matching **blue trapezoids** for each of 10 **Blocks**.)

3. Follow Steps 8 and 9 of **Assembling the Quilt Top**, page 105, to make 20 **Unit 1's** and 20 **Unit 2's**.

4. Using **squares** and red and blue print **strips**, follow Steps 10 - 13 of **Assembling the Quilt Top**, page 105, to make 10 **Unit 3's**.

5. Follow Steps 15 - 17 of **Assembling the Quilt Top**, page 106, to complete 10 **Blocks**.

6. Referring to **Wall Hanging Top Diagram**, sew **Blocks** together to make center section of wall hanging top.

7. Follow **Adding Mitered Borders**, page 118, to add borders to center section to complete **Wall Hanging Top**.

8. Follow **Quilting**, page 118, to mark, layer, and quilt using **Quilting Diagram**, page 106, as a suggestion. Our wall hanging is hand quilted.

9. Follow **Making a Hanging Sleeve**, page 124, to attach hanging sleeve to wall hanging back.

9. Cut a 22" square of binding fabric. Follow **Binding**, page 122, to bind wall hanging using 2¹/₂"w bias binding with mitered corners.

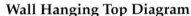

Wall Hanging Top Diagram

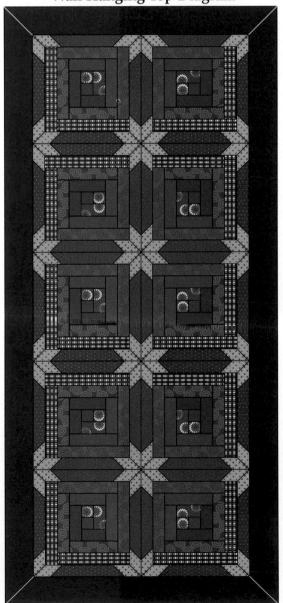

GENERAL INSTRUCTIONS

Complete instructions are given for making each of the quilts and other projects shown in this book. Skill levels indicated for quilts and wall hangings may help you choose the right project. To make your quilting easier and more enjoyable, we encourage you to carefully read all of these general instructions, study the color photographs, and familiarize yourself with the individual project instructions before beginning a project.

QUILTING SUPPLIES

This list includes all the tools you need for basic quick-method quiltmaking, plus additional supplies used for special techniques. Unless otherwise specified, all items may be found in your favorite fabric store or quilt shop.

Batting — Batting is most commonly available in polyester, cotton, or a polyester/cotton blend (see **Choosing and Preparing the Batting**, page 120).

Cutting mat — A cutting mat is a special mat designed to be used with a rotary cutter. A mat that measures approximately 18" x 24" is a good size for most cutting.

Eraser — A soft white fabric eraser or white art eraser may be used to remove pencil marks from fabric. Do not use a colored eraser, as the dye may discolor fabric.

Iron — An iron with both steam and dry settings and a smooth, clean soleplate is necessary for proper pressing.

Marking tools — There are many different types of marking tools available (see **Marking Quilting Lines**, page 119). A silver quilter's pencil is a good marker for both light and dark fabrics.

Masking tape — Two widths of masking tape, 1"w and 1/4"w, are helpful to have when quilting. The 1"w tape is used to secure the backing fabric to a flat surface when layering the quilt. The 1/4"w tape may be used as a guide when outline quilting.

Needles — Two types of needles are used for hand sewing: *Betweens*, used for quilting, are short and strong for stitching through layered fabric and batting. *Sharps* are longer, thinner needles used for basting and other hand sewing. For *sewing machine needles*, we recommend size 10 to 14 or 70 to 90 universal (sharp-pointed) needles.

Paper-backed fusible web — This iron-on adhesive with paper backing is used to secure fabric cutouts to another fabric when appliquéing. If the cutouts will be stitched in place, purchase a lighter weight web that will not gum up your sewing machine needle. A heavier weight web is used for appliqués that are fused in place with no stitching.

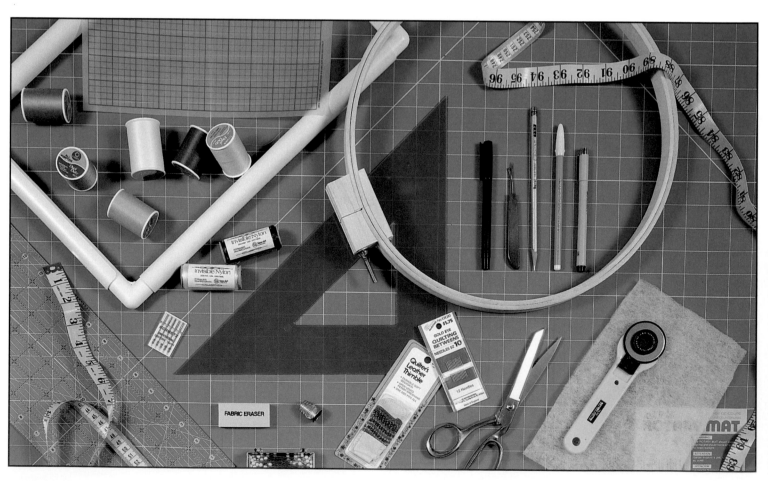

Permanent fine-point marker — A permanent marker is used to mark templates and stencils and to sign and date quilts. Test marker on fabric to make sure it will not bleed or wash out.

Pins — Straight pins made especially for quilting are extra long with large, round heads. Glass head pins will stand up to occasional contact with a hot iron. Some quilters prefer extra-fine dressmaker's silk pins. If you are machine quilting, you will need a large supply of 1" long (size 01) rust-proof safety pins for pin-basting.

Quilting hoop or frame — Quilting hoops and frames are designed to securely hold the 3 layers of a quilt together while you quilt. Many different types and sizes are available, including round and oval wooden hoops, frames make of rigid plastic pipe, and large floor frames made of either material. A 14" or 16" hoop allows you to quilt in your lap and makes your quilting portable.

Rotary cutter — The rotary cutter is the essential tool for quick-method quilting techniques. The cutter consists of a round, sharp blade mounted on a handle with a retractable blade guard for safety. It should be used only with a cutting mat and rotary cutting ruler. Two sizes are generally available; we recommend the large (45 mm) size.

Rotary cutting ruler — A rotary cutting ruler is a thick, clear acrylic ruler made specifically for use with a rotary cutter. It should have accurate 1/8" crosswise and lengthwise markings and markings for 45° and 60° angles. A 6" x 24" ruler is a good size for most cutting. An additional 6" x 12" ruler or 12 1/2" square ruler is helpful when cutting wider pieces. Many specialty rulers are available that make specific cutting tasks faster and easier.

Scissors — Although most cutting will be done with a rotary cutter, sharp, high-quality scissors are still needed for some cutting. A separate pair of scissors for cutting paper and plastic is recommended. Smaller scissors are handy for clipping threads.

Seam ripper — A good seam ripper with a fine point is useful for removing stitching.

Sewing machine — A sewing machine that produces a good, even straight stitch is all that is necessary for most quilting. Zigzag stitch capability is necessary for **Almost Invisible Appliqué**, page 116. Clean and oil your machine often and keep the tension set properly.

Stabilizer — Commercially made non-woven material or paper stabilizer is placed behind background fabric when doing **Almost Invisible Appliqué**, page 116, to provide a more stable stitching surface.

Tape measure — A flexible 120" long tape measure is helpful for measuring a quilt top before adding borders.

Template material — Sheets of translucent plastic, often pre-marked with a grid, are designed especially for making templates and quilting stencils.

Thimble — A thimble is necessary when hand quilting. Thimbles are available in metal, plastic, or leather and in many sizes and styles. Choose a thimble that fits well and is comfortable.

Thread — Several types of thread are used for quiltmaking: *General-purpose* sewing thread is used for basting, piecing, and some appliquéing. Buy high-quality cotton or cotton-covered polyester thread in light and dark neutrals, such as ecru and grey, for your basic supplies. *Quilting* thread is stronger than general-purpose sewing thread, and some brands have a coating to make them slide more easily through quilt layers. Some machine appliqué projects in this book use *transparent monofilament* (clear nylon) thread. Use a very fine (.004 mm), soft nylon that is not stiff or wiry. Choose clear nylon thread for white or light fabrics or smoke nylon thread for darker fabrics.

Triangle — A large plastic right-angle triangle (available in art and office supply stores) is useful in rotary cutting for making first cuts to "square up" raw edges of fabric for checking to see that cuts remain at right angles to the fold.

Walking foot — A walking foot or even-feed foot is needed for straight-line machine quilting. This special foot will help all 3 layers of the quilt to move at the same rate over the feed dogs to provide a smoother quilted project.

FABRICS
SELECTING FABRICS

For many quilters, choosing fabric for a new quilt project is one of the most fun, yet most challenging, parts of quiltmaking. Photographs of our quilts are excellent guides for choosing the colors for your quilt. You may choose to duplicate the colors in the photographs, or you may use the same light, medium, and dark values in completely different color families. When you change the light and dark value placement in a quilt block, you may come up with a surprising new creation. The most important lesson to learn about fabrics and color is to choose fabrics you love. When you combine several fabrics you are simply crazy about in a quilt, you are sure to be happy with the results!

The yardage requirements listed for each project are based on 45" wide fabric with a "usable" width of 42" after shrinkage and trimming selvages. Your actual usable width will probably vary slightly from fabric to fabric. Though most fabrics will yield 42" or more, if you find a fabric that you suspect will yield a narrower usable width, you will need to purchase additional yardage to compensate. Our recommended yardage lengths should be adequate for occasional resquaring of fabric when many cuts are required, but it never hurts to buy a little more fabric for insurance against a narrower usable width, the occasional cutting error, or to have on hand for making coordinating projects.

Choose high-quality, medium-weight, 100% cotton fabrics such as broadcloth or calico. All-cotton fabrics hold a crease better, fray less, and are easier to quilt than cotton/polyester blends. All the fabrics for a quilt should be of comparable weight and weave. Check the end of the fabric bolt for fiber content and width.

PREPARING FABRICS

All fabrics should be washed, dried, and pressed before cutting.

1. To check colorfastness before washing, cut a small piece of the fabric and place in a glass of hot water with a little detergent. Leave fabric in the water for a few minutes. Remove from water and blot fabric with white paper towels. If any color bleeds onto the towels, wash the fabric separately with warm water and detergent, then rinse until the water runs clear. If fabric continues to bleed, choose another fabric.

2. Unfold yardage and separate fabrics by color. To help reduce raveling, use scissors to snip a small triangle from each corner of your fabric pieces. Machine wash fabrics in warm water with a small amount of mild laundry detergent. Do not use fabric softener. Rinse well and then dry fabrics in the dryer, checking long fabric lengths occasionally to make sure they are not tangling.

3. To make ironing easier, remove fabrics from dryer while they are slightly damp. Refold each fabric lengthwise (as it was on the bolt) with wrong sides together and matching selvages. If necessary, adjust slightly at selvages so that fold lies flat. Press each fabric with a steam iron set on "Cotton."

ROTARY CUTTING

*Based on the idea that you can easily cut strips of fabric and then cut those strips into smaller pieces, rotary cutting has brought speed and accuracy to quiltmaking. Observe safety precautions when using the rotary cutter since it is extremely sharp. Develop a habit of retracting the blade guard **just before** making a cut and closing it **immediately afterward**, before laying down the cutter.*

1. Follow **Preparing Fabrics** to wash, dry, and press fabrics.

2. Cut all strips from the selvage-to-selvage width of the fabric unless otherwise indicated. Place fabric on the cutting mat as shown in **Fig. 1** with the fold of the fabric toward you. To straighten the uneven fabric edge, make the first "squaring up" cut by placing the right edge of the rotary cutting ruler over the left raw edge of the fabric. Place right-angle triangle (or another rotary cutting ruler) with the lower edge carefully aligned with the fold and the left edge against the ruler (**Fig. 1**). Hold the ruler firmly with your left hand, placing your little finger off the left edge to anchor the ruler. Remove the triangle, pick up the rotary cutter, and retract the blade guard. Using a smooth, downward motion, make the cut by running the blade of the rotary cutter firmly along the right edge of the ruler (**Fig. 2**). **Always** cut in a direction **away** from your body and **immediately** close the blade guard after each cut.

Fig. 1

Fig. 2

3. To cut each of the strips required for the project, place the ruler over the cut edge of the fabric, aligning desired marking on the ruler with the cut edge (**Fig. 3**), and then make the cut. When cutting several strips from a single piece of fabric, it is important to occasionally use the ruler and triangle to ensure that cuts are still at a perfect right angle to the fold. If not, repeat Step 2 to straighten.

Fig. 3

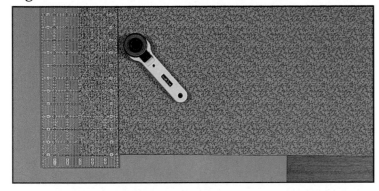

4. To square up selvage ends of a strip before cutting pieces, refer to **Fig. 4** and place folded strip on a mat with selvage ends to your right. Aligning a horizontal marking on ruler with 1 long edge of strip, use rotary cutter to trim off selvage to make end of strip square and even (**Fig. 4**). Turn strip (or entire mat) so that cut end is to your left before making subsequent cuts.

Fig. 4

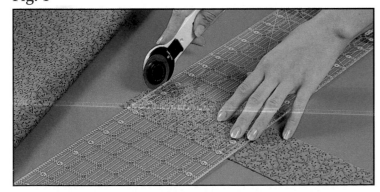

5. Pieces such as rectangles and squares can now be cut from strips. (Cutting other shapes such as diamonds is discussed in individual project instructions.) Usually strips remain folded, and pieces are cut in pairs after ends of strips are squared up. To cut squares or rectangles from a strip, place ruler over left end of strip, aligning desired marking on ruler with cut end of strip. To ensure perfectly square cuts, align a horizontal marking on ruler with 1 long edge of strip (**Fig. 5**) before making the cut.

Fig. 5

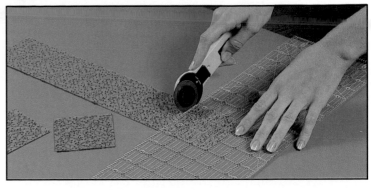

6. To cut 2 triangles from a square, cut square the size indicated in the project instructions. Cut square once diagonally to make 2 triangles (**Fig. 6**).

Fig. 6

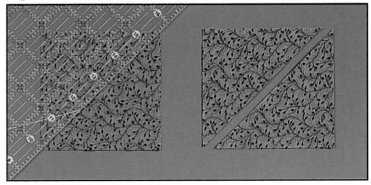

7. To cut 4 triangles from a square, cut square the size indicated in the project instructions. Cut square twice diagonally to make 4 triangles (**Fig. 7**). You may find it helpful to use a small rotary cutting mat so that the mat can be turned to make second cut without disturbing fabric pieces.

Fig. 7

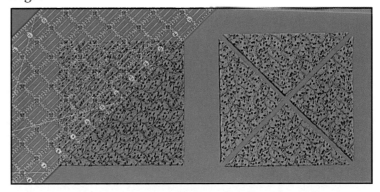

8. After some practice, you may want to try stacking up to 6 fabric layers when making cuts. When stacking strips, match long cut edges and follow Step 4 to square up ends of strip stack. Carefully turn stack (or entire mat) so that squared-up ends are to your left before making subsequent cuts. After cutting, check accuracy of pieces. Some shapes, such as diamonds, are more difficult to cut accurately in stacks.

9. In some cases, strips will be sewn together into strip sets before being cut into smaller units. When cutting a strip set, align a seam in strip set with a horizontal marking on the ruler to maintain square cuts (**Fig. 8**). We do not recommend stacking strip sets for rotary cutting.

Fig. 8

10. Most borders for quilts in this book are cut along the more stable lengthwise grain to minimize wavy edges caused by stretching. To remove selvages before cutting lengthwise strips, place fabric on mat with selvages to your left and squared-up end at bottom of mat. Placing ruler over selvage and using squared-up edge instead of fold, follow Step 2, page 112, to cut away selvages as you did raw edges (**Fig. 9**). After making a cut the length of the mat, move the next section of fabric to be cut onto the mat. Repeat until you have removed selvages from required length of fabric.

Fig. 9

11. After removing selvages, place ruler over left edge of fabric, aligning desired marking on ruler with cut edge of fabric. Make cuts as in Step 3. After each cut, move next section of fabric onto mat as in Step 10.

TEMPLATE CUTTING

Our full-sized piecing templates have 2 lines: a solid cutting line and a dashed line showing the ¼" seam allowance.

1. To make a template from a pattern, use a permanent fine-point marker to carefully trace pattern onto template plastic, making sure to transfer all alignment and grain line markings. Cut out template along inner edge of drawn line. Check template against original pattern for accuracy.

2. To use a template, place template on wrong side of fabric, aligning grain line on template with straight grain of fabric. Use a sharp fabric marking pencil to draw around template. Transfer all alignment markings to fabric. Cut out fabric piece using scissors or rotary cutter and ruler.

PIECING AND PRESSING

Precise cutting, followed by accurate piecing and careful pressing, will ensure that all the pieces of your quilt top fit together well.

PIECING

Set sewing machine stitch length for approximately 11 stitches per inch. Use a new, sharp needle suited for medium-weight woven fabric.

Use a neutral-colored general-purpose sewing thread (not quilting thread) in the needle and in the bobbin. Stitch first on a scrap of fabric to check upper and bobbin thread tension; make any adjustments necessary.

For good results, it is **essential** that you stitch with an **accurate** ¼" seam allowance. On many sewing machines, the measurements from the needle to the outer edge of the presser foot is ¼". If this is the case with your machine, the presser foot is your best guide. If not, measure ¼" from the needle and mark with a piece of masking tape. Special presser feet that are exactly ¼" wide are also available for most sewing machines.

When piecing, **always** place pieces **right sides together** and **match raw edges**; pin if necessary. (If using straight pins, remove the pins just before they reach the sewing machine needle.)

Chain Piecing

Chain piecing whenever possible will make your work go faster and will usually result in more accurate piecing. Stack the pieces you will be sewing beside your machine in the order you will need them and in a position that will allow you to easily pick them up. Pick up each pair of pieces, carefully place them together as they will be sewn, and feed them into the machine one after the other. Stop between each pair only long enough to pick up the next and don't cut thread between pairs (**Fig. 10**). After all pieces are sewn, cut threads, press, and go on to the next step, chain piecing when possible.

Fig. 10

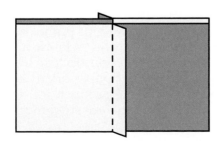

Sewing Strip Sets

When there are several strips to assemble into a strip set, first sew the strips together into pairs, then sew the pairs together to form the strip set. To help avoid distortion, sew 1 seam in 1 direction and then sew the next seam in the opposite direction (**Fig. 11**).

Fig. 11

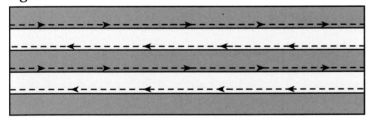

Sewing Across Seam Intersections

When sewing across the intersection of 2 seams, place pieces right sides together and match seams exactly, making sure seam allowances are pressed in opposite directions (**Fig. 12**). To prevent fabric from shifting, you may wish to pin in place.

Fig. 12

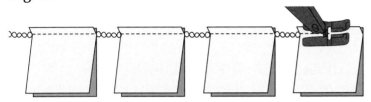

Sewing Sharp Points

To ensure sharp points when joining triangular or diagonal pieces, stitch across the center of the "X" (shown in pink) formed on the wrong side by previous seams (**Fig. 13**).

Fig. 13

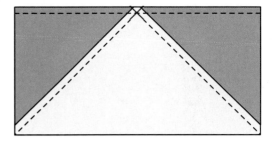

Sewing Bias Seams

Care should be used in handling and stitching bias edges since they stretch easily. After sewing the seam, carefully press seam allowances to 1 side, making sure not to stretch the fabric.

Making Triangle-Squares

The grid method for making triangle-squares is faster and more accurate than cutting and sewing individual triangles. Stitching before cutting the triangle-squares apart also prevents stretching the bias edges.

1. Follow project instructions to cut rectangles or squares of fabric for making triangle-squares. Place the indicated pieces right sides together and press.
2. On the wrong side of the lighter fabric, draw a grid of squares similar to that shown in **Fig. 14**. The size and number of squares will be given in the project instructions.

Fig. 14

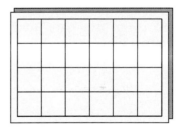

3. Following the example given in the project instructions, draw 1 diagonal line through each square in the grid (**Fig. 15**).

Fig. 15

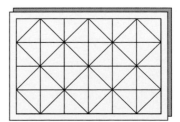

4. Stitch ¼" on each side of all diagonal lines. For accuracy, it may be helpful to first draw your stitching lines onto the fabric, especially if your presser foot is not your ¼" guide. In some cases, stitching may be done in a single continuous line. Project instructions include a diagram similar to **Fig. 16**, which shows stitching lines and the direction of the stitching.

Fig. 16

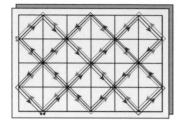

5. Use rotary cutter and ruler to cut along all drawn lines of the grid. Each square of the grid will yield 2 triangle-squares (**Fig. 17**).

Fig. 17

6. Carefully press triangle-squares open, pressing seam allowances toward darker fabric. Trim off points of seam allowances that extend beyond edges of triangle-square (see **Fig. 18**).

Trimming Seam Allowances
When sewing with diamond or triangle pieces, some seam allowances may extend beyond the edges of the sewn pieces. Trim away "dog ears" that extend beyond the edges of the sewn pieces (**Fig. 18**).

Fig. 18

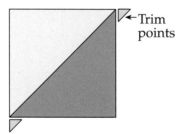

Trim points

PRESSING
Use a steam iron set on "Cotton" for all pressing. Press as you sew, taking care to prevent small folds along seamlines. Seam allowances are almost always pressed to one side, usually toward the darker fabric. However, to reduce bulk it may occasionally be necessary to press seam allowances toward the lighter fabric or even to press them open. In order to prevent a dark fabric seam allowance from showing through a light fabric, trim the darker seam allowance slightly narrower than the lighter seam allowance. To press long seams, such as those in long strip sets, without curving or other distortion, lay strips across the width of the ironing board.

APPLIQUÉ
PREPARING APPLIQUÉ PIECES
Patterns are printed in reverse to enable you to use our speedy method of preparing appliqués. White or light-colored fabrics may need to be lined with fusible interfacing before applying fusible web to prevent darker fabrics from showing through.

1. Place paper-backed fusible web, web side down, over appliqué pattern. Use a pencil to trace pattern onto paper side of web as many times as indicated in project instructions for a single fabric. Repeat for additional patterns and fabrics.
2. Follow manufacturer's instructions to fuse traced patterns to wrong side of fabrics. Do not remove paper backing.
3. Some projects may have pieces that are given as measurements (such as a 2" x 4" rectangle) instead of drawn patterns. Fuse web to wrong side of the fabrics indicated for these pieces.
4. Use scissors to cut out appliqué pieces along traced lines; use rotary cutting equipment to cut out appliqué pieces given as measurements. Remove paper backing from all pieces.

ALMOST INVISIBLE APPLIQUÉ
This method of appliqué is an adaptation of satin stitch appliqué that uses clear nylon thread to secure the appliqué pieces. Transparent monofilament (clear nylon) thread is available in 2 colors: clear and smoke. Use clear on white or very light fabrics and smoke on darker colors.

1. Referring to diagram and/or photo, arrange appliqués on the background fabric and follow manufacturer's instructions to fuse in place.
2. Pin a stabilizer, such as paper or any of the commercially available products, on wrong side of background fabric before stitching appliqués in place.
3. Thread sewing machine with transparent monofilament thread; use general-purpose thread that matches background fabric in bobbin.

4. Set sewing machine for a very narrow width (approximately 1/16") zigzag stitch and a short stitch length. You may find that loosening the top tension slightly will yield a smoother stitch.

5. Begin by stitching 2 or 3 stitches in place (drop feed dogs or set stitch length at 0) to anchor thread. Most of the zigzag stitch should be done on the appliqué with the right edges of the stitch falling at the very outside edge of the appliqué. Stitch over all exposed raw edges of appliqué pieces.

6. (*Note:* Dots on **Figs. 19 - 24** indicate where to leave needle in fabric when pivoting.) For **outside corners**, stitch just past the corner, stopping with the needle in **background** fabric (**Fig. 19**). Raise presser foot. Pivot project, lower presser foot, and stitch adjacent side (**Fig. 20**).

Fig. 19   **Fig. 20**

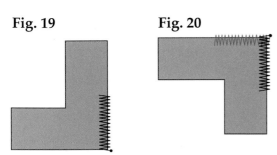

7. For **inside corners**, stitch just past the corner, stopping with the needle in **appliqué** fabric (**Fig. 21**). Raise presser foot. Pivot project, lower presser foot, and stitch adjacent side (**Fig. 22**).

Fig. 21   **Fig. 22**

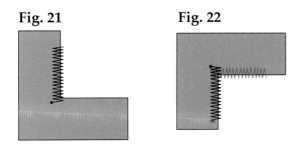

8. When stitching **outside** curves, stop with needle in **background** fabric. Raise presser foot and pivot project as needed. Lower presser foot and continue stitching, pivoting as often as necessary to follow curve (**Fig. 23**).

Fig. 23

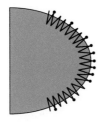

9. When stitching **inside** curves, stop with needle in **appliqué** fabric. Raise presser foot and pivot project as needed. Lower presser foot and continue stitching, pivoting as often as necessary to follow curve (**Fig. 24**).

Fig. 24

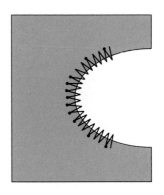

10. Do not backstitch at end of stitching. Pull threads to wrong side of background fabric; knot thread and trim ends.

11. Carefully tear away stabilizer.

BORDERS

Borders cut along the lengthwise grain will lie flatter than borders cut along the crosswise grain. In most cases, our instructions for cutting borders for bed-size quilts include an extra 2" of length at each end for "insurance"; borders will be trimmed after measuring completed center section of quilt top.

ADDING SQUARED BORDERS

1. Mark the center of each edge of quilt top.

2. Squared borders are usually added to top and bottom, then side edges of the center section of a quilt top. To add top and bottom borders, measure across center of quilt top to determine length of borders (**Fig. 25**). Trim top and bottom borders to the determined length.

Fig. 25

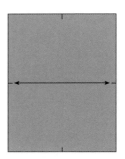

3. Mark center of 1 long edge of top border. Matching center marks and raw edges, pin border to quilt top, easing in any fullness; stitch. Repeat for bottom border.
4. Measure center of quilt top, including attached borders, to determine length of side borders. Trim side borders to the determined length. Repeat Step 3 to add borders to quilt top (**Fig. 26**).

Fig. 26

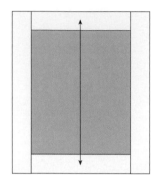

ADDING MITERED BORDERS

1. Mark the center of each edge of quilt top.
2. Mark center of 1 long edge of top border. Measure across center of quilt top (see **Fig. 25**). Matching center marks and raw edges, pin border to center of quilt top edge. Beginning at center of border, measure 1/2 the width of the quilt top in both directions and mark. Match marks on border with corners of quilt top and pin. Easing in any fullness, pin border to quilt top between center and corners. Sew border to quilt top between center and corners. Sew border to quilt top, beginning and ending seams **exactly** 1/4" from each corner of quilt top and backstitching at beginning and end of stitching (**Fig. 27**).

Fig. 27

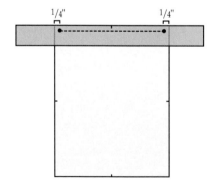

3. Repeat Step 2 to sew bottom, then side borders, to center section of quilt top. To temporarily move first 2 borders out of the way, fold and pin ends as shown in **Fig. 28**.

Fig. 28

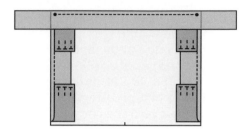

4. Fold 1 corner of quilt top diagonally with right sides together and matching edges. Use ruler to mark stitching line as shown in **Fig. 29**. Pin borders together along drawn line. Sew on drawn line, backstitching at beginning and end of stitching (**Fig. 30**).

Fig. 29   **Fig. 30**

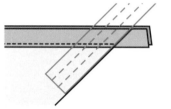   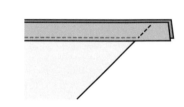

5. Turn mitered corner right side up. Check to make sure corner will lie flat with no gaps or puckers.
6. Trim seam allowance to 1/4"; press to 1 side.
7. Repeat Steps 4 - 6 to miter each remaining corner.

QUILTING

Quilting holds the 3 layers (top, batting, and backing) of the project together and can be done by hand or machine. Our project instructions tell you which method is used on each project and show you quilting diagrams that can be used as suggestions for marking quilting designs. Because marking, layering, and quilting are interrelated and may be done in different orders depending on circumstances, please read this entire section, pages 118 - 122, before beginning the quilting process on your project.

TYPES OF QUILTING

In the Ditch

Quilting very close to a seamline (**Fig. 31**) or appliqué (**Fig. 32**) is called "in the ditch" quilting. This type of quilting does not need to be marked and is indicated on our quilting diagrams with blue lines close to seamlines. When quilting in the ditch, quilt on the side **opposite** the seam allowance.

Fig. 31   **Fig. 32**

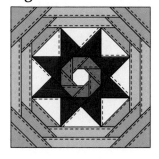

Outline Quilting

Quilting approximately ¼" from a seam or appliqué is called "outline" quilting (**Fig. 33**). This type of quilting is indicated on our quilting diagrams by blue lines a short distance from seamlines. Outline quilting may be marked, or you may place ¼"w masking tape along seamlines and quilt along the opposite edge of the tape. (Do not leave tape on project longer than necessary, since it may leave an adhesive residue.)

Fig. 33

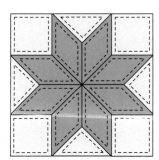

Ornamental Quilting

Quilting decorative lines or designs is called "ornamental" quilting (**Fig. 34**). Ornamental quilting is indicated on our quilting diagrams by blue lines. This type of quilting should be marked before you baste project layers together.

Fig. 34

MARKING QUILTING LINES

Fabric marking pencils, various types of chalk markers, and fabric marking pens with inks that disappear with exposure to air or water are readily available and work well for different applications. Lead pencils work well on light-colored fabrics, but marks may be difficult to remove. White pencils work well on dark-colored fabric, and silver pencils show up well on many colors. Since chalk rubs off easily, it's a good choice if you are marking as you quilt. Fabric marking pens make more durable and visible markings, but the marks should be carefully removed according to manufacturer's instructions. Press down only as hard as necessary to make a visible line.

When you choose to mark your quilt, whether before or after the layers are basted together, is also a factor in deciding which marking tool to use. If you mark with chalk or a chalk pencil, handling the project during basting may rub off the markings. Intricate or ornamental designs may not be practical to mark as you quilt; mark these designs before basting using a more durable marker.

To choose marking tools, take all these factors into consideration and **test** different markers **on scrap fabric** until you find the one that gives the desired result.

USING QUILTING STENCILS

A wide variety of pre-cut stencils, as well as entire books of quilting patterns, are available at your local quilt shop or fabric store. Wherever you draw your quilting inspiration from, using a stencil makes it easier to mark intricate or repetitive designs on your quilt top.

1. To make a stencil from a pattern, center template plastic over pattern and use a permanent marker to trace pattern onto plastic.
2. Use a craft knife with a single or double blade to cut narrow slits along traced lines (**Fig. 35**).

Fig. 35

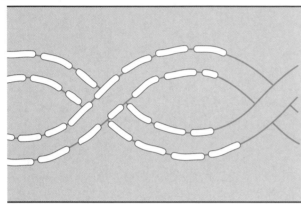

3. Use desired marking tool and stencil to mark quilting lines.

CHOOSING AND PREPARING THE BACKING

To allow for slight shifting of the quilt top during quilting, the backing should be approximately 4" larger on all sides for a bed-size quilt top or approximately 2" larger on all sides for a wall hanging. Yardage requirements listed for quilt backings are calculated for 45"w fabric. If you are making a bed-size quilt, using 90"w or 108"w fabric for the backing may eliminate piecing. To piece a backing using 45"w fabric, use the following instructions.

1. Measure length and width of quilt top; add 8" (4" for a wall hanging) to each measurement.
2. If quilt top is 76"w or less, cut backing fabric into 2 lengths slightly longer than the determined **length** measurement. Trim selvages. Place lengths with right sides facing and sew long edges together, forming a tube (**Fig. 36**).

Fig. 36

3. Match seams and press along 1 fold (**Fig. 37**).

Fig. 37

4. Cut along pressed fold to form a single piece (**Fig. 38**).

Fig. 38

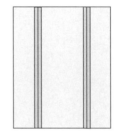

5. If quilt top is more than 76"w, cut backing fabric into 3 lengths slightly longer than the determined **width** measurement. Trim selvages. Sew long edges together to form a single piece.
6. Trim backing to correct size, if necessary, and press seam allowances open.

CHOOSING AND PREPARING THE BATTING

Choosing the right batting will make your quilting job easier. For fine hand quilting, choose a low-loft batting in any of the fiber types described here. Machine quilters will want to choose a low-loft batting that is all cotton or a cotton/polyester blend because the cotton helps "grip" the layers of the quilt. If the quilt is to be tied, a high-loft batting, sometimes called extra-loft or fat batting, is a good choice.

Batting is available in many different fibers. Bonded polyester batting is one of the most popular batting types. It is treated with a protective coating to stabilize the fibers and to reduce "bearding," a process where batting fibers work their way out through the quilt fabrics. Other batting options include cotton/polyester batting, which combines the best of both polyester and cotton batting; all-cotton batting, which must be quilted more closely than polyester batting; and wool and silk battings, which are generally more expensive and are usually only dry-cleanable.

Whichever batting you choose, read the manufacturer's instructions closely for any special notes on care or preparation. When you're ready to use your chosen batting in a project, cut the batting the same size as the prepared backing.

LAYERING THE QUILT

1. Examine wrong side of quilt top closely; trim any seam allowances and clip any threads that may show through the front of the quilt. Press quilt top.
2. If quilt top is to be marked before layering, mark quilting lines (see **Marking Quilting Lines**, page 119).
3. Place backing **wrong** side up on a flat surface. Use masking tape to tape edges of backing to surface. Place batting on top of backing fabric. Smooth batting gently, being careful not to stretch or tear. Center quilt top **right** side up on batting.
4. If hand quilting, begin in the center and work toward the outer edges to hand baste all layers together. Use long stitches and place basting lines approximately 4" apart (**Fig. 39**). Smooth fullness or wrinkles toward outer edges.

Fig. 39

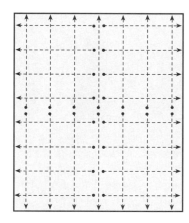

5. If machine quilting, use 1" rust-proof safety pins to "pin-baste" all layers together, spacing pins approximately 4" apart. Begin at the center and work toward the outer edges to secure all layers. If possible, place pins away from areas that will be quilted, although pins may be removed as needed when quilting.

HAND QUILTING

The quilting stitch is a basic running stitch that forms a broken line on the quilt top and backing. Stitches on the quilt top and backing should be straight and equal in length.

1. Secure center of quilt in hoop or frame. Check quilt top and backing to make sure they are smooth. To help prevent puckers, always begin quilting in the center of the quilt and work toward the outside edges.

2. Thread needle with an 18" - 20" length of quilting thread; knot 1 end. Using a thimble, insert needle into quilt top and batting approximately 1/2" from where you wish to begin quilting. Bring needle up at the point where you wish to begin (**Fig. 40**); when knot catches on quilt top, give thread a quick, short pull to "pop" knot through fabric into batting. (**Fig. 41**).

Fig. 40

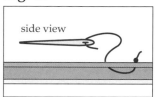

side view

Fig. 41

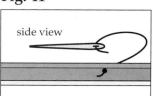

side view

3. Holding the needle with your sewing hand and placing your other hand underneath the quilt, use thimble to push the tip of the needle down through all layers. As soon as needle touches your finger underneath, use that finger to push the tip of the needle only back up through the layers to top of quilt. (The amount of the needle showing above the fabric determines the length of the quilting stitch.) Referring to **Fig. 42**, rock the needle up and down, taking 3 - 6 stitches before bringing the needle and thread completely through the layers. Check the back of the quilt to make sure stitches are going through all layers. When quilting through a seam allowance or quilting a curve or corner, you may need to take 1 stitch at a time.

Fig. 42

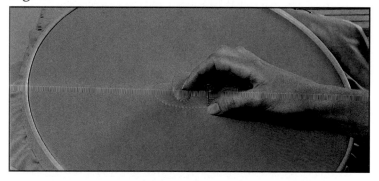

4. When you reach the end of your thread, knot thread close to the fabric and "pop" knot into batting; clip thread close to fabric.
5. Stop and move your hoop as often as necessary. You do not have to tie a knot every time you move your hoop; you may leave the thread dangling and pick it up again when you return to that part of the quilt.

MACHINE QUILTING

The machine-quilted projects in this book feature straight-line quilting, which requires a walking foot or even-feed foot. The term "straight-line" is somewhat deceptive, since curves (especially gentle ones), as well as straight lines, can be stitched with this technique.

1. Wind your sewing machine bobbin with general-purpose thread that matches the quilt backing. Do not use quilting thread. Thread the needle of your machine with transparent monofilament thread if you want your quilting to blend with your quilt top fabric. Use decorative thread, such as a metallic or contrasting-colored general-purpose thread, when you want the quilting lines to stand out more. Set the stitch length for 6 - 10 stitches per inch and attach the walking foot to sewing machine.

2. After pin-basting, decide which section of the quilt will have the longest continuous quilting line, oftentimes the area from center top to center bottom. Leaving the area exposed where you will place your first line of quilting, roll up each edge of the quilt to help reduce the bulk, keeping fabrics smooth. Smaller projects may not need to be rolled.

3. Start stitching at beginning of longest quilting line, using very short stitches for the first 1/4" to "lock" beginning of quilting line. Stitch across project, using one hand on each side of the walking foot to slightly spread the fabric and to guide the fabric through the machine. Lock stitches at end of quilting line.

4. Continue machine quilting, stitching the longer quilting lines first to stabilize the quilt before moving on to other areas.

BINDING

Binding encloses the raw edges of your quilt. Because of its stretchiness, bias binding works well for binding projects with curves or rounded corners and tends to lie smooth and flat in any given circumstance. It is also more durable than other types of binding. Binding may also be cut from the straight lengthwise or crosswise grain of the fabric. You will find that straight-grain binding works well for projects with straight edges.

MAKING CONTINUOUS BIAS STRIP BINDING

Bias strips for binding can simply be cut and pieced to the desired length. However, when a long length of binding is needed, the "continuous" method is quick and accurate.

1. Cut a square from binding fabric the size indicated in the project instructions. Cut square in half diagonally to make 2 triangles.

2. With right sides together and using a 1/4" seam allowance, sew triangles together (**Fig. 43**); press seam allowance open.

Fig. 43

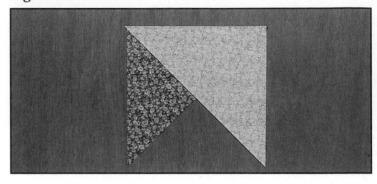

3. On wrong side of fabric, draw lines the width of the binding as specified in the project instructions, usually 2½" (**Fig. 44**). Cut off any remaining fabric less than this width.

Fig. 44

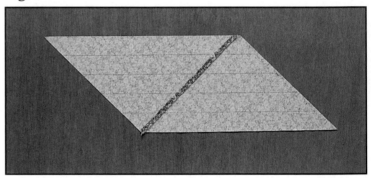

4. With right sides inside, bring short edges together to form a tube; match raw edges so that first drawn line of top section meets second drawn line of bottom section (**Fig. 45**).

Fig. 45

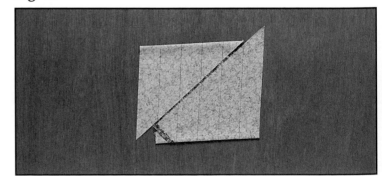

5. Carefully pin edges together by inserting pins through drawn lines at the point where drawn lines intersect, making sure the pins go through intersections on both sides. Using a ¼" seam allowance, sew edges together. Press seam allowances open.

6. To cut continuous strip, begin cutting along first drawn line (**Fig. 46**). Continue cutting along drawn line around tube.

Fig. 46

7. Trim ends of bias strip square.

8. Matching wrong sides and raw edges, press bias strip in half lengthwise to complete binding.

MAKING STRAIGHT-GRAIN BINDING

1. To determine length of strip needed if attaching binding with mitered corners, measure edges of the quilt and add 12".

2. To determine lengths of strips needed if attaching binding with overlapped corners, measure each edge of quilt; add 3" to each measurement.

3. Cut lengthwise or crosswise strips of binding fabric the determined length and the width called for in the project instructions. Strips may be pieced to achieve the necessary length.

4. Matching wrong sides and raw edges, press strip(s) in half lengthwise to complete binding.

ATTACHING BINDING WITH MITERED CORNERS

1. Press 1 end of binding diagonally (**Fig. 47**).

Fig. 47

2. Beginning with pressed end several inches from a corner, lay binding around quilt to make sure that seams in binding will not end up at a corner. Adjust placement if necessary. Matching raw edges of binding to raw edge of quilt top, pin binding to right side of quilt along 1 edge.

3. When you reach the first corner, mark ¼" from corner of quilt top (**Fig. 48**).

Fig. 48

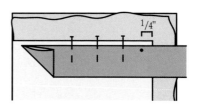

4. Using a ¼" seam allowance, sew binding to quilt, backstitching at beginning of stitching and when you reach the mark (**Fig. 49**). Lift needle out of fabric and clip thread.

Fig. 49

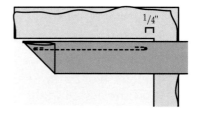

5. Fold binding as shown in **Figs. 50** and **51** and pin binding to adjacent side, matching raw edges. When you reach the next corner, mark ¼" from edge of quilt top.

Fig. 50   **Fig. 51**

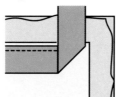   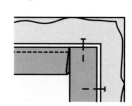

6. Backstitching at edge of quilt top, sew pinned binding to quilt (**Fig. 52**); backstitch when you reach the next mark. Lift needle out of fabric and clip thread.

Fig. 52

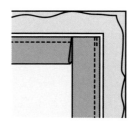

7. Repeat Steps 5 and 6 to continue sewing binding to quilt until binding overlaps beginning end by approximately 2". Trim excess binding.

8. Trim backing and batting a scant 1/4" larger than quilt top so that batting and backing will fill the binding when it is folded over to the quilt backing.
9. On 1 edge of quilt, fold binding over to quilt backing and pin pressed edge in place, covering stitching line (**Fig. 53**). On adjacent side, fold binding over, forming a mitered corner (**Fig. 54**). Repeat to pin remainder of binding in place.

Fig. 53   **Fig. 54**

10. Blindstitch binding to backing, taking care not to stitch through to front of quilt.

ATTACHING BINDING WITH OVERLAPPED CORNERS
1. Matching raw edges and using a 1/4" seam allowance, sew a length of binding to top and bottom edges on right side of quilt.
2. Trim backing and batting from top and bottom edges a scant 1/4" larger than quilt top so that batting and backing will fill the binding when it is folded over to the quilt backing.
3. Trim ends of top and bottom binding even with edges of quilt top. Fold binding over to quilt backing and pin pressed edges in place, covering stitching line (**Fig. 55**); blindstitch to backing.

Fig. 55

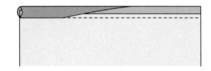

4. Leaving approximately 1½" of binding at each end, stitch a length of binding to each side edge of quilt. Trim backing and batting as in Step 2.
5. Trim each end of binding ½" longer than bound edge. Fold each end of binding over to quilt backing (**Fig. 56**); pin in place. Fold binding over to quilt backing and blindstitch in place, taking care not to stitch through to front of quilt.

Fig. 56

MAKING A HANGING SLEEVE

Attaching a hanging sleeve to the back of your wall hanging or quilt before the binding is added allows you to display your completed project on a wall.

1. Measure the width of the wall hanging top and subtract 1". Cut a piece of fabric 7"w by the determined measurement.
2. Press short edges of fabric piece 1/4" to wrong side; press edges 1/4" to wrong side again and machine stitch in place.
3. Matching wrong sides, fold piece in half lengthwise to form a tube.
4. Follow project instructions to sew binding to quilt top and to trim backing and batting. Before blindstitching binding to backing, match raw edges and stitch hanging sleeve to center top edge on back of wall hanging.
5. Finish binding wall hanging, treating the hanging sleeve as part of the backing.
6. Blindstitch bottom of hanging sleeve to backing, taking care not to stitch through to front of quilt.
7. Insert dowel or slat into hanging sleeve.

PILLOW FINISHING
MAKING THE PILLOW
1. For pillow back, cut a piece of fabric the same size as pieced and quilted pillow top.
2. Add welting or ruffle to pillow top if indicated in project instructions (see below).
3. Place pillow back and pillow top right sides together. Using a 1/4" seam allowance (or stitching as close as possible to welting), sew pillow top and back together, leaving an opening at bottom edge for turning. Turn pillow right side out, carefully pushing corners outward. Stuff with polyester fiberfill or pillow form and sew final closure by hand.

ADDING WELTING
1. To make welting, measure outer dimensions of pillow top and add 2". Cut a bias strip of fabric the width specified in project instructions, equal in length to determined measurement, piecing if necessary.
2. Lay cord along center of bias strip on wrong side of fabric; fold strip over cord. Using a zipper foot, machine baste along length of strip close to cord. Trim seam allowance to 1/2".
3. Matching raw edges and beginning and ending 3" from ends of welting, baste welting to right side of pillow top. To make turning corners easier, clip seam allowance of welting at pillow top corners.

4. Remove approximately 3" of seam at 1 end of welting, fold fabric away from cord. Trim remaining end of welting so that cord ends meet exactly. Fold short edge of welting fabric ½" to wrong side; fold fabric back over area where ends meet (**Fig. 57**) Baste remainder of welting to pillow top close to cord.

Fig. 57

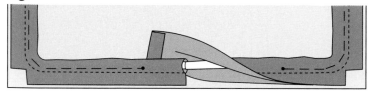

5. Follow Step 3 of **Making the Pillow** to complete pillow.

ADDING A RUFFLE
1. To determine length of ruffle fabric, measure outer dimensions of pillow top and multiply by 2. To determine width of ruffle fabric, multiply the finished width measurement given in project instructions by 2 and add 1". Cut a strip of fabric the determined measurements, piecing if necessary.
2. Matching right sides, use a ¼" seam allowance to sew short edges of ruffle together to form a large circle; press seam allowance open. To fold ruffle in half, match raw edges and fold 1 raw edge of fabric to inside of circle to meet remaining raw edge of fabric; press.
3. To gather ruffle, place quilting thread ¼" from raw edge of ruffle. Using a medium width zigzag stitch with medium stitch length, stitch over quilting thread, being careful not to catch quilting thread in stitching. Pull quilting thread, drawing up gathers to fit pillow top.
4. Matching raw edges, baste ruffle to right side of pillow top.
5. Follow Step 3 of **Making The Pillow**, to complete pillow.

EMBROIDERY STITCHES
BLANKET STITCH
Come up at 1, go down at 2, and come up at 3, keeping thread below point of needle (**Fig. 58**). Continue working as shown in **Fig. 59**.

Fig. 58

Fig. 59

SIGNING AND DATING YOUR QUILT

Your completed quilt is a work of art and should be treated as such. And like any artist, you should sign and date your work. There are many different ways to do this, and you should pick a method of signing and dating that reflects the style of the quilt, the occasion for which it was made, and your own particular talents.

The following suggestions may give you an idea for recording the history of your quilt for future generations.

- Embroider your name, the date, and any additional information on the quilt top or backing. You may choose floss colors that closely match the fabric you are working on, such as white floss on a white border, or contrasting colors may be used.
- Make a label from muslin and use a permanent marker to write your information. Your label may be as plain or as fancy as you wish. Then stitch the label to the back of the quilt.
- Chart a cross-stitch label design that includes the information you wish and stitch it in colors that complement the quilt. Stitch the finished label to the quilt backing.

GLOSSARY

Appliqué — A cutout fabric shape that is secured to a larger background. Also refers to the technique of securing the cutout pieces.

Backing — The back or bottom layer of a quilt, sometimes called the "lining."

Backstitch — A reinforcing stitch taken at the beginning and end of a seam to secure stitches.

Basting — Large running stitches used to temporarily secure pieces or layers of fabric together. Basting is removed after permanent stitching.

Batting — The middle layer of a quilt that provides the insulation and warmth as well as the thickness.

Bias — The diagonal (45° for true bias) grain of fabric in relation to crosswise or lengthwise grain (see **Fig. 60**).

Binding — The fabric strip used to enclose the raw edges of the layered and quilted quilt. Also refers to the technique of finishing quilt edges in this way.

Blindstitch — A method of hand sewing an opening closed so that it is invisible.

Border — Strips of fabric that are used to frame a quilt top.

Chain piecing — A machine-piecing method consisting of joining pairs of pieces one after the other by feeding them through the sewing machine without cutting the thread between the pairs.

Grain — The direction of the threads in woven fabric. "Crosswise grain" refers to the threads running from selvage to selvage. "Lengthwise grain" refers to the threads running parallel to the selvages (**Fig. 60**).

Fig. 60

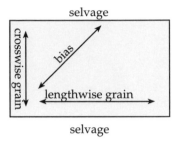

Machine baste — To baste using a sewing machine set at a long stitch length.

Miter — A method used to finish corners of quilt borders or bindings consisting of joining fabric pieces at a 45° angle.

Piecing — Sewing together the pieces of a quilt design to form a quilt block or an entire quilt top.

Pin basting — Using rust-proof safety pins to secure the layers of a quilt together prior to machine quilting.

Quilt blocks — Pieced or appliquéd sections that are sewn together to form a quilt top.

Quilt top — The decorative part of a quilt that is layered on top of the batting and backing.

Quilting — The stitching that holds together the 3 quilt layers (top, batting, and backing); or, the entire process of making a quilt.

Running stitch — A series of straight stitches with the stitch length equal to the space between stitches (**Fig. 61**).

Fig. 61

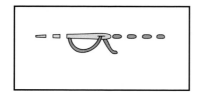

Sashing — Strips or blocks of fabric that separate individual blocks in a quilt top.

Seam allowance — The distance between the seam and the cut edge of the fabric. In quilting, the seam allowance is usually 1/4".

Selvages — The 2 finished lengthwise edges of fabric (see **Fig. 59**). Selvages should be trimmed from fabric before cutting.

Set (or Setting) — The arrangement of the quilt blocks as they are sewn together to form the quilt top.

Setting squares — Squares of plain (unpieced) fabric set between pieced or appliquéd quilt blocks in a quilt top.

Setting triangles — Triangles of fabric used around the outside of a diagonally-set quilt top to fill in between outer squares and border or binding.

Stencil — A pattern used for marking quilting lines.

Straight grain — The crosswise or lengthwise grain of fabric (see **Fig. 60**). The lengthwise grain has the least amount of stretch.

Strip set — Two or more strips of fabric that are sewn together along the long edges and then cut apart across the width of the sewn strips to create smaller units.

Template — A pattern used for marking quilt pieces to be cut out.

Triangle-square — In piecing, 2 right triangles joined along their long sides to form a square with a diagonal seam (**Fig. 62**).

Fig. 62

Unit — A pieced section that is made as individual steps in the quilt construction process are completed. Units are usually combined to make blocks or other sections of the quilt top.